MW00882739

# THERE THERE NOW

## A Memoir

Carol Wolleson

*To
Best wishes
from Carol
11/10/18*

Copyright © 2018 by Carol Wolleson

All rights reserved

*Library of Congress Cataloging-in-Publication Data is available.*
ISBN-13:  978-1718866539
ISBN-10:  1718866534

Cover design by Alex Hammarstedt

Cover photo and sculpture by Steve Gillman

Author photo by Lewis S. Mudge

*To my family, no matter what they think of my memoir.*

There's no there there.
> —Gertrude Stein in painful
> acknowledgement that her
> childhood home in Oakland had
> been torn down (*Everybody's
> Autobiography*, 1937).

## NOTE TO READER

*Carol shares her truth here with humor and bravery. Hers is not a celebrity memoir, written to impress. She divulges dirt on herself that many of us have but most of us hide.*

*You might see that she spent a chunk of time being her own worst enemy but conquered herself to become her own friend. You might recognize that her courage has made her life rich. You might acknowledge that all her stumbles paved the way to her career as a therapist.*

*I see that the publishing of her memoir is another in a long line of Carol's helpful acts—helping herself and her audience. When I read her words, I laugh, I cry, and I laugh again. She highlights our common plights and triumphs. By sharing her ordeals, she makes them ordinary and more survivable for us all, bringing us closer to home.*

*I hope you grow from her truth.*

> —Laura E. Miller, Editor
> Oakland, April 18, 2018

# THERE THERE NOW

## Why I Write

The 60s and 70s were a time of personal growth, creativity, and a time to crack open and expose prejudice and repression. I dropped halfway out, usually keeping a job. À la mode, I stopped shaving my armpits and legs. I did my share of tripping, protesting the war, naked dancing, and making candles and yogurt and macramé plant-hangers. My adventures led me deep into psychotherapy and to a career as a therapist in the San Francisco Bay Area. This was a leap from my upbringing in the 40s and 50s as the daughter of a commercial fisherman and an at-home mom in the insular fishing and logging town of Astoria, Oregon.

Before I settled down and got to the task of taking myself seriously, I careened through the times. I collected experiences that begged to be told, but I trace the genesis of my writing life to a magazine enticement when I was eight years old. Ballpoint pens had just become available and a manufacturer tapped into my youthful ambition by rewarding successful door-to-door sales with a new pen.

My mother helped me order the kit—a small punchboard with about twenty sealed cells, each containing a tightly rolled up slip of paper I could punch out. Only one punch won the ballpoint pen. I would sell chances to win a pen, and as CEO I would earn one too. The punchboard did not cost anything so there was little risk. This was something new and exciting; I was confident I could sell out the board and get my coveted pen.

I enjoyed knocking on neighbors' doors and inviting them to pay a nickel a chance. It was a small town and my customers knew who I was and where I lived, so they trusted me with their investment. The punchboard sold out fast. I sent in the money and waited for the promised pens. They soon arrived and I dutifully delivered one to the winner. The pen was shiny light blue metal and was as thick in the barrel as rope. It leaked indelible blue ink all over my hand and the page, but the novelty made up for the mess. I used this wonderful invention until it ran dry.

Memoir is memory. I recall the manufacturer's name on our family bathtub and our first phone number from seventy years ago, but I usually draw a blank when it comes to recalling family events. I rely on my sister who is the family Google. She can recall who was there, the weather at the time (an ever-present topic in Oregon), what we had to eat, and who said what to whom. It's like hearing a vaguely interesting story about another family. She's the authority on that history. But if you want a testimonial about bathtub fixtures from Wolverine Brass Works in Grand Rapids, Michigan, try me on 1995-R. You'll have to get an operator first.

I hope when I'm old my wits will not have been crowded out by ancient phone numbers or bathtub makes. And when I can't do much except sit and think, I hope I have a clear perspective. That's the gift of very old age—sitting still. Writing a memoir is a lot like returning from a long trip abroad. The trip is always better when you return home, unpack, clean up, rest up, and look at your photos.

# Passing Go
# (Childhood to College)

In the fall it's rainy and dark. The hanging flower baskets overflowing with purple and pink petunias along the main street are gone, and the town is a gray, uninviting place. I was embarrassed when my friends from Oakland arrived on just such a fall day. They might see me as drab and colorless too.

But when the sun is out it's a sparkly place, as if the town had been waiting for a charge and been jolted alive. The immense Columbia River it sits beside sparkles. The cruise ships on their way to Alaska send us visitors who have lots of sparkly money to brighten the moods of shopkeepers. The artfully painted Victorians smile and proudly puff out their verandas, showing off their historical markers like a piece of jewelry. The houses are spaced for easy walking, one to the next, as though placed by a winning Monopoly player. The shiny black granite walls of the Maritime Memorial honor those who made their living on the river and the sea.

Today, it's a museum town. Gone are the twenty or more hard-working fish canneries. You always knew when they were canning tuna. You would be assaulted by a fishy odor almost as bad as the rotten-eggs smell of pulp mills farther up the river. But it was a reassuring smell. It meant that fisherman had successful catches, and the Finnish cannery ladies had work. It smelled like money, only fishy. The saunas would stay open and the taverns would be full.

In a period of unemployment in my thirties I stayed with my parents for a few weeks, and to amuse myself I put on a sociologist's hat and explored. In a town of about ten thousand people, I counted twenty-three bars and taverns. I counted about the same number of jewelry stores. Interesting. Then I saw the symbiotic relationship. After a successful catch, men would go out and get drunk. Their wives would be furious. Husbands would then buy jewelry, seeking forgiveness. Both taverns and jewelry stores did well.

When I was growing up, no business could have survived without at least one Finnish-speaking employee there at all times, so numerous were the Finnish immigrants who could not speak English. I loved their lilting names—Kumpela, Lempea, Sarvinen, Hautala, Niemi. Has anyone set those names to music? Most Finnish homes had a sauna (pronounced sow-nuh, not saw-nuh) in the basement of their homes.

Besides the canneries, gone too are the native Chinook people and the early fur traders, and, later, the U.S. Navy sailors based nearby and the loggers risking their lives in the woods. The town seemed rough to me as a kid, with its loggers, fishermen and sailors. You were tagged "sailor bait" if you dated one. That meant "cheap."

The city was too poor to keep the blackberries from overgrowing the few tennis courts, but it did maintain an outdoor pool where everybody swam, except during the polio epidemic. No one knew how polio spread, but one theory was by water. So we sunbathed on our roof instead, deep-frying ourselves with baby oil and went to the beach as often as Mom would drive us the ten miles to Peter Iredale Beach or Seaside.

We of course took for granted the endless, silky sand beaches and the Pacific Ocean that was our playground. All this richness, and I could not wait to get away as soon as I got the chance. Now I love visiting—when the sun is out and it all sparkles.

My visiting friends from California are the kindest of people. They know me well and know I am not drab. Even so, I protected my home town by peppering my guests with so much history on a whirlwind tour to all the notable sites they could not possibly have formed anything but a favorable impression.

## Our House

We moved to Irving Avenue in Astoria when I was six. My father proudly paid six thousand dollars in cash for our new house. It had been built with a view of the Columbia River by a river pilot. The flagpole was a ship's mast, the mailbox a bronze binnacle (direction finder) from a ship. The pink concrete walkway up to the house just inside the white picket fence had a legend in blue concrete: *Cave Canum* (beware of the dog). The eccentric captain put it in Latin so as not to insult his dog. Even though we did not have a dog, the words in the cement walk remained. Not a single other home in town had Latin on a sidewalk and I knew it. The words made us special. Cultured. I murmured them to myself every time I returned home and opened the gate in the white picket fence. I would murmur these foreign words to myself, and I felt oddly excited. *Cave canum* did not only mean "beware of the dog." To me it hinted at the immensity of the world outside the picket fence.

Nautical features were continued inside. We climbed the narrow, vertical stairs, imitating a ship's ladder, to the finished attic. We hoisted ourselves up the ladder hanging onto a thick, white rope, shiny and smooth with use. The stairs were concealed by a cupboard door in the hallway. Unlike civil clock bells, a ship's clock chimes eight bells at 4:00 p.m., 8:00 p.m., midnight, and 4:00 a.m. to signal a new four-hour watch aboard a ship. For example, 4:30 p.m. is one bell, 5:00 is two bells, 5:30 is three bells, adding another bell each half hour until arriving at 8 p.m. with eight bells. Then the sequence starts again. Lots of bells. The essential barometer hung in the alcove near the desk. A perfect house for a fisherman's family.

Perfect except that it had only one bathroom and there were five of us. My younger sister Sharon would lock herself in the bathroom on school mornings and take a very long time to get ready. Patti and I would pound on the door for our turn. I think it was one of the few ways Sharon, the youngest, could assert herself. By the time we were ready for school everyone was mad.

My parents lived in the house almost all of their fifty years of marriage. When I was last in Astoria I drove by the house, stopped, and knocked on the door. The new owner graciously let me go through the house. I declined a climb up the ladder to the attic. She had made almost no changes inside, but vandals had chipped the distinctive bronze binnacle-mailbox from its concrete pier and stolen it.

My father and I were buddies. With my mother I was stubborn, angry, distant, and sometimes loving. I spent years in therapy working my way out of that morass. Some psychologist wag once said we spend our entire adult lives trying to come to terms with our childhood.

My mother told me that when I was born the first thing I did was look all around the room, taking in the world with my new blue eyes. Unspoken might have been that I did not immediately seek her out. I think we always had a weak bond. As a teen I was inspecting myself in the mirror and found a small, round scar at my throat. In horror I showed my mother, fearing it was ringworm. She burst into tears. She had been holding me when I was a baby, smoking, and dropped her cigarette on me, leaving a faint scar. I think she hoped I would never find it.

I am three years old and on the steamer moving from Alaska to Seattle with my mother and baby sister. My father is coming down on his boat. Some nights it's rough and I'm seasick. I'm in the top bunk and have to climb down the steep ladder by myself to be sick in the basin. My mother is trying to sleep with the baby in her arms. She's sick too and can't help me down the ladder. I hang on tight.

My father is to catch up with us, bringing his boat alongside the steamer so that my mother can toss his forgotten shaving kit down to him. She must do this

9

at just the right moment. He is balancing on the top of the hold on the main deck. The boat pitches and rocks. I watch, fearful he may lose his balance or that my mother will miss and the kit will be lost overboard. Or that maybe both of them will fall overboard. Or that I will.

As an adult when I tell my mother this story she is dumbfounded. This experience I remember with such vivid details never happened. It's my turn to be dumbfounded. When I thought about it, of course it wasn't possible. How could they find each other in the open water? How could a small fishing boat catch up with a large steamer? How could he bring the boat in close enough without damaging it?

I was a three-year-old novelist translating my fears of separation and loss into a story I later told and retold. I still like to think it actually happened.

I'm not yet four years old. I remember walking hand in hand with my mother on a sunny day and hanging back fearfully when I see a large hole in the sidewalk. She asks me what is wrong, and I say I am afraid I will fall into that hole. She laughs and explains it is only a shadow, not a hole in the sidewalk. I think she marveled to have a glimpse into her child's mind. I remember being surprised that one moment I saw a gaping, black chasm and the next a solid sidewalk in shadow. I remember clearly seeing the shift. I knew I had accomplished something significant. I was seeing the world as it really was. Shadows would no longer scare me.

On another sunny day, perhaps two years later, I am sitting in my red wagon on the sidewalk in front of our house. A woman walks by and comments, "What a pretty little girl." I reply sourly and emphatically, "I am not." I remember wondering why I was so grumpy with her. I must have been angry about something with my mother or sisters, and my unhappy self snarled at the hapless passerby instead of the real culprits.

We children each had our own way of disposing of our vegetables. I dropped carrots in my milk. Sharon threw peas on the floor. Patti hid hers under her plate. I don't know if Mom knew what we were doing during dinner. I'm surprised we weren't called back after dinner to eat another serving when she discovered the milky carrots, the mashed peas on the floor as she cleared the table. Actually, I think she was amused by our stealthy cleverness. I don't think she liked the boiled carrots and peas either.

When I was six I had appendicitis. I was playing at Janice's house when suddenly I knew I had to go home. My stomach hurt really bad. I knew it was different from an ordinary stomachache. My mother knew just what to do. Before she married she had worked at Children's Hospital in Seattle. She didn't drive so she called a taxi and we sped down the hill to the hospital. The nurses rushed me into surgery and my near-to-bursting appendix was removed. This was two days before my sixth birthday. On April 5 the nurses proudly wheeled in on a tall food cart my birthday cake—candles, singing, and presents. I felt bad that I couldn't eat it. I didn't want to disappoint them. But everything tasted vile, like the ether I had been given, a commonly used anesthetic at the time. Back at home recovering, I was told not to walk very much. But I would sneak short steps around the living room when no one was looking because it was so much fun to walk and feel so stiff around my middle.

The first time I remember clearly feeling my mother's warmth was when I went to town by myself and needed to phone her about something. I was about nine or ten. I was surprised how soft and sweet her voice sounded. I heard love and caring in her voice. I picked a weed on the way home to give to her. A single stalk, the head was lacy and graceful. I told her it reminded me of her. I hoped she understood. I was trying to tell her I loved her.

She had one doll from her childhood. She let me play with it occasionally. One day I cracked its ceramic head. She had been very poor, and this was the only treasured thing she had from her childhood. I saw her tears. She did not scold me, just told me softly it was all right. I think she saw my guilty, stricken face when I told her.

My father spent many hours building the dollhouse he gave me for Christmas one year. He had recently paid cash for the first and only house he ever bought. What better way to express his pride than to build a replica for his eldest daughter?  The same glossy white cedar shakes, red roof and trim. He and Slim, our next-door neighbor, designed and built the dollhouse in Slim's basement. I think that's the only project they ever did together. Slim was in the Navy and was transferred to another base.

My mother spent many fall evenings making furniture for the dollhouse out of cardboard and cotton batting. A wing chair and a green sofa with cushions resembled the furniture in our living room. She was a careful crafter; no raw edges or stray threads. She found a plastic dining set, buffet and china closet which imitated our imitation, post-war Hepplewhite. Miniature beds and dressers for the bedrooms.

This was a gift of the Magi. I can imagine the loving hours, their anticipation of my excitement. There was only one problem. They had moved the dollhouse to our basement shortly before Christmas Eve when it was to be unveiled. In the time-honored tradition of childhood at Christmastime, I had been snooping and found it. It was covered with a blanket but was too large to conceal completely. I had guessed it was for me. Snooping was one thing, but you're not supposed to actually see the gift. I knew I had done something awful. When they brought the dollhouse into the living room on Christmas Eve, bursting with pride, I must have responded with a flat, quiet thank you. Heavy with guilt, I couldn't pretend to be excited. I hope I cried. I remember their confusion, their disappointment. I think my mother understood what had happened. I hope she understood how guilty I felt. I'm sure my mother was hurt, but she hid hers better than my father. My father could not hide his hurt. I hope she was able to help him understand what had gone wrong.

I hope my father saw later what a potent thing he had created. The dollhouse was the focus of intense play with my friends and two sisters and, later, for their grandchildren.

My best friend Maureen was going to Amato's nightclub with her parents for her ninth birthday and invited me to go with her. Her parents were older than most of my friends' parents and Maureen was a bit odd, but I thought it was the most unimaginably exciting thing to be invited to go out to a nightclub. We would have dinner and dance to an orchestra. When my mother said no, I let loose with my best wailing and whining, hoping I could wear her down. Her "no" was so obviously unjust. She had no basis for it, except to say that it was a school night and, besides, children didn't go to nightclubs. I wondered at the time if she was jealous. Maybe she had never been to Amato's.

My father was home from fishing at the time. I appealed to him. I begged and pleaded. I could see him considering my case as I wove frantically around them in the kitchen. Finally, he said, softly, "Well, Agnes, I don't see why she can't go." Maureen's parents were well-known in town. Her father owned a jewelry store on Commercial Street with the respectable hyphenated name of Loop-Jacobson Jewelers. I would be in good hands.

I remember my mother tightening her lips in disapproval, but she gave in. This was my first taste of my mother's discomfort with the slightest hint of sexuality. Now I can follow her thinking: A nightclub is where people go to drink. Probably dance too close together. Maybe go to the car or home with a stranger and do who-knows-what. She could see only the seamy side.

The big day arrived. I began dancing around the house as soon as I got home from school. My mother's continuing disapproval could not dampen my excitement. I wore my best dress and hair bow and patent leather Mary Janes.

Mr. and Mrs. Loop picked me up at six o'clock. Amato's was empty when we arrived to claim our table at the edge of the dance floor. It was too early for all that dangerous nightlife my mother envisioned. Although it was early, the band played, the lighting dimmed. I don't think Maureen's parents danced. She and I had the dance floor to ourselves. We whirled round and round. Her parents watched us fondly. I wish mine had been there to see how lovely and innocent it was.

My mother told me a story which explained a lot about the sometimes troubled maternal relationships in my family. When she was small and walking in the dark with her own mother from the henhouse to the farmhouse in a lightning storm, crying, terribly frightened, my grandmother snorted and said, "Do you think I can stop the lightning?" and trudged on with her eggs, leaving the little girl, my mother, trying to catch up with her, shivering in fright. Her mother was not especially nurturing, leaving my mother with a nurturing deficit which she then passed on to me. When I was perhaps eleven or twelve, my mother did a surprising thing. She took us to stay overnight at a nearby beach town. An adventure for her and us three girls. I had to share a double bed with her. I was uncomfortable with this, and I hugged the edge of the bed all night fearing I would disturb her. I think I was a bit afraid of my mother and needed to keep my distance. I did not even consider this an opportunity to snuggle with her. In the morning, she seemed surprised and puzzled when she said I had hardly moved all night. I think she recognized how uneasy I was being that close to her.

I ache for the physical nurturing she needed and did not get and for my need to be enfolded and comforted by her.

My mother is sitting on the edge of her bed attempting to repair a run in her stockings. The precious gossamer nylon stockings, fragile as cobwebs. Precious because it is wartime and nylon is tightly rationed. Nylon had replaced silk. I don't know where my mother got such a prize, rarer than butter, sugar, leather. These things were scarce at home so that soldiers in Europe would have food and boots. I think my father had given the stockings to her as a gift

The least tug could open a run and ruin a stocking. She is trying to salvage hers, and her hopes, by using a special hooked needle to relink the ladder of unsightly, ruined stitches. I am seven years old. I am leaning close against my mother, trying to see. I sense in her intense concentration these stockings are something special. I am holding my breath as though the least puff of air might snag them.

My father was away on the ocean for weeks at a time. When he was in port he was busy, and tired. This night, they are going dancing, a rare occasion. I can sense my mother is happy, yet tense. She is determined to wear her precious gift stockings. I see for the first time that my mother is a young woman, a person separate from me. For the first time, I see she is more than Mother. She is a young wife who wants to be beautiful for her husband. She wants her legs to feel silky and smooth as she dances with my father, who danced seldom but danced well. She wants to please him. It is vital she repair her stockings. They promise romance, desire. I am confused, a little afraid. I think it is something I am not ready to know, but I already do know. My mother is now changed for me. For the first time, I see my father as more than just my father. My mother loves him and sometimes he will be first in her heart. I must share my mother with him. He will sometimes come between us. My mother and I will never be as close as we were before I saw her mending her stockings.

It was a summer Sunday. We were all out mowing and edging the lawn. The radio was balanced on the sill of an open window, the volume raised. We would stay close to the radio listening for news of the men trying to dig out three-year-old Kathy Fiscus who had fallen a hundred feet down the shaft of an abandoned water well in San Marino, California. It was national news. The tension was terrible. Then we heard she was dead when they reached her after three days trapped in the well. That night and every night before bedtime for several weeks I would go through our entire house, basement to attic, checking to make sure every door and every window was secure and locked. I did not stop to wonder what I was doing. I just had to do it. My parents never said a word. I wondered why they did not, but I did not want them to stop me either. I know they understood the fear I felt, that we all felt, listening to this event unfolding. I was afraid one of us would wander out and fall down a well. Recently, I looked up the girl's name on the Internet and found the story. The events were just as I remember. I also learned that it was her father who had dug the well.

If it was a sunny Sunday and my father was home, we would pack a picnic and head to the closest trout stream. He was the only one who fished; it was the thing he loved the most. While my mother read and my father fished, we three girls would explore the woods and the stream. I had gone alone into the woods lining the edge of the small stream when I came to a large boulder. I climbed up, lay down on the warm rock, and looked down into a wide, deep pool of still water. The sun cast patches of light and shadow through trees arching over the pool. I lay there dreaming. I knew this place was special because most of the stream was narrow and shallow and here was this mysterious deep pool. I wanted to stay all afternoon, but I was eager to show my mother this amazing discovery. I carefully marked the spot where I came out of the woods and ran across the field to where my mother sat reading on the picnic blanket. I led her back to the spot I had marked, through the woods to the stream bank.

It wasn't there. No boulder; no deep, still pool; no arching tree boughs; no sanctuary. Frantic, near tears, I searched up and down the stream. I couldn't find it. Then it was time to go home.

It was inconceivable to me that I had imagined the quiet, shady perch over a mysterious pool in a trout stream. It had to be real. I was there. But it was not to be found.

Perhaps I needed that day to create my world as the most beautiful place I could possibly imagine. In my mind I go there still, to the warm boulder, lie down on my belly and dream gazing into the soothing, deep waters of the pool in the trout stream.

I believe that experiences of childhood are remembered when that miniature self, the observing ego, appears, a scribe noting important events for future use. Actually, I'll call it my observing angel, because she's led me through and out of many a psychic swamp with her stories.

Mother's closet was almost empty, preferring to buy us girls beautiful clothes rather than spend the family's limited budget on herself. People always told us how well-dressed we were. Every August she would take us to Portland to shop for school clothes.

August in Portland is hot, but we went from store to store to find just the right stuff, all of us dripping with perspiration, especially my mother who was very sensitive to heat. We three were her art project, her canvas. I thank her for giving me good taste and a sense of style. She was frugal but not with her daughters. Much later I took Mother on a bus trip through the British Isles and to Paris for a few days. To shop, of course. I tried on a pair of strange-looking shoes, gray-blue Arche sandals, very expensive, very French. I hesitated. Mother urged me to buy them. She was more adventurous than I.

My mother had wanted to work when I was in high school but my father objected. In those days, it was inferred that a man could not support his family if his wife worked. She thought she might work in a gift shop, like her friend Ellen. Ellen was her one close friend until my father and Ellen's husband Bud had an argument. Bud had done something my father thought was illegal or morally indefensible and told Bud so. They never spoke again and that ended my mother's only close friendship. I know her life was lonely. She spent much of it waiting for my father to come home. I was too preoccupied with my own loneliness to notice hers.

My fourteenth year changed the course of my life.

Eighth grade, and I had finally arrived at the inner circle of the most popular girls. Earlier in junior high during recess I would hide in a restroom stall and read because I didn't know how to make friends. I would

20

stand on the toilet so I wouldn't be discovered. Girls knew I was there anyway. One day a girl yanked open the door and exposed me. Yelled something taunting at me.

But now I was friends with Charlotte, Nancy, Patty, Billie Ann, and Carol. Especially Carol, who was top girl. I was thrilled when I was invited by Carol and her family to go on an overnight boat trip to Deep River for Fourth of July. When we returned Carol and I wanted to go to a movie. Her mother asked if it was okay with my mother. I lied and said yes. So we went. When we returned, Carol's mother had discovered my lie and accused me, with venom in her voice. She had been drinking. I lost my temper. I yelled at her. I swore at her. She called my mother, who arrived a few minutes later, as grim as I had ever seen her. I asked Carol if we could still be friends and she said she didn't know.

I went immediately to bed, shaking and miserable. My mother said nothing. I knew she was upset but I didn't know what kind of upset. Angry? Humiliated? Disappointed? And where did all my rage come from? I didn't know it was there.

For the rest of the summer I babysat every afternoon. All my friends disappeared. No phone calls, no going to the pool, no invitation to movies. I felt doomed. I was dying inside. The isolation was unbearable. Finally, I couldn't stand it any longer and called Billie Ann and asked her to do something with me. She said her mother wouldn't let her. I didn't believe her. It was really because she was in deep with Carol and did not want to risk the coveted friendship.

At fourteen, friends are the most important thing in the world. Despair was not too strong a word to describe my feelings. I was facing my freshman year without a friend. I constructed a shell around myself, a shell which smiled and went through the motions of joining clubs, becoming a cheerleader, even joining a high school sorority. But inside I was aching. I held my head up high. To hold myself together I had to become stiff. Sometimes after school when no one was home, I would lean against the dining room table and cry. After football and basketball games I would drift off into the darkness toward home rather than hike with the other kids up the hill to the after-game dances.

For over a year I agonized, trying to work up my courage to apologize to Carol's mother. I would walk toward her house and then veer away, paralyzed with guilt and fear. Finally, one day, quivering, I rang her doorbell. She was at home vacuuming. She turned her machine off, briefly. I managed to say I was sorry and started to cry. I don't remember what she said. She nodded curtly and motioned for me to leave, restarting her vacuum before I was out the door. I felt no sense of forgiveness but was relieved it was over. I know I behaved better than she did.

My mother never talked to me about what had happened. Her stoic Norwegian upbringing warned against talking about anything difficult or emotional. It would have helped so much if she had taken me in her arms and let me cry it out. The only time she mentioned it was when I told her many years later I had started therapy. She said, "Oh, Carol, I'm so glad.

In high school, you were so withdrawn and we were very worried about you."

I had no idea.

The incident with Carol's mother was a defining moment in my life. I had no resources to cope with all that emotional trauma, and my fourteen-year-old self could not reason her way back to emotional health. Without some encouragement from my mother, I couldn't confide in her. There was no grandmother, no nearby aunt, no caring neighbor to help me with the awful guilt and help me fend off depression. I built a thick wall around myself and pretended to be okay. In fact, I was deeply depressed. I did not begin to tear down that wall until I started therapy almost twenty years later.

My mother and I clashed. In high school, I would yell at her, "I hate you, I hate you," and later, almost on my knees by her bed, say I was sorry. She would respond, coldly, "All right." I knew I had hurt her deeply. We didn't cry and hug. I would leave her bedroom unforgiven, feeling even more wretched. I don't remember what I was so angry about. So much unspoken pain was bottled up within each of us.

I was guarded with my mother. I couldn't confide in her; I kept my distance. Only much later in my life I recognized that she was the one who encouraged me to achieve. In her firm but gentle way she reminded me for six years to practice piano daily for an hour. She encouraged me to try things even when they were scary. She refinished a desk and chair for my bedroom and kept my younger sisters quiet so I could study in the evening. She wanted me to have a comfortable, attractive place to study. In high school when I was desperate for friends she let me stop piano lessons so I could be a cheer leader. I was an accomplished pianist, and I know it was painful for my mother to let me stop. She saw my desperation. She was the one who insisted I go to college, not my father. Even though he had attended university briefly, it did not occur to him to send his daughter to school. He saw me only in a blurry, besotted way. My mother appraised me and recognized that I was capable.

In adulthood we repaired our relationship, treating each other with the loving kindness and gentleness we both longed for, the hateful words replaced with words of caring. She died in 2001 from Alzheimer's complications. I still miss her.

My father was an albacore fisherman for over fifty years. Scientists tell us that tuna bones, at least forty-two thousand years old, were discovered recently in a cave in East Timor. Does this finding make fishing the oldest profession in the world?

My father wrote his memoirs about his adventurous years of deep sea fishing but not a word about the mystery and beauty of the sea. He was not a Homer, poet of the wine-dark sea. It is indeed wine-dark; I saw it myself sailing through the Greek islands. My sailing adventures were brief, only a day between ports. My father would be on the ocean for two to three weeks at a time, trolling the Pacific Ocean from Canada to Mexico. There was no mention in his memoirs of the phosphorescent glow of the water at night, exotic birds, mysterious surges of waves and wind. Perhaps poetic words were unnecessary. His half century on the ocean attests to his romance.

He was proud of his ability to meet the might of the ocean with all his strength and wits, and survive it. He was confident enough in his sixty-foot boat, the Argo (namesake of the ship of Jason and the Argonauts) to head out even when a storm was predicted. He didn't tell his daughters what it was like in the open ocean riding out sixty-mile-an-hour winds and heaving troughs of water in a historic October storm. My mother did not tell him how frightened in our beds we were as we heard the wind howling in the eaves of our house. Once he miscalculated in thick fog and collided with a jetty as he navigated into an unfamiliar port. To hear him tell it, the placement of the jetty was a personal insult to his seamanship. Although the damage to the Argo was considerable, he was able to get her to a dock.

To protect us children he abbreviated his stories. Even now I'm not sure I could stand to hear their retelling in full. We suspected that every time he came home from a trip he had escaped death. This was never spoken aloud.

But we children would dramatize it. We would jump up and down every time he came home from fishing. For that matter, we did this even when he was in port and went to work on the boat every day. My mother only once showed her displeasure with our exuberance. She did not want to be reminded that we were dancing with joyous relief because he had come home once again.

We were dancing, too, because we could have some fun with our dad. He would tease, and we would flirt. We had another audience for our stories. I remember the need for attention from him, knowing our time with him was limited. He would be leaving again soon, and we would see him only briefly when he came in to unload the tuna, reload with groceries, and head out. He would be gone most of the summer and some years even into November when the albacore was especially abundant.

When he was home for the winter he was always up early, eager to get to the Argo. There was the Atlas diesel engine, the Sonar, the Freon, the painting. Everything needed oiling, repairing, replacing. His greatest need was for engine rags. A big bag of clean rags was his favorite Christmas present. The oily, dark green Atlas engine seemed to occupy most of the hold and require most of the rags. I was always nervous climbing down the ladder, squeezing past the pulsing engine along the narrow passageway leading to the galley and four bunks. The huge spinning flywheel had no protective cover; even the slender pistons pumping up and down seemed dangerous. What if the boat lurched and I were suddenly thrown onto the flywheel or into the pulsing pistons?

Today this monster of an engine, no longer oily, is the first exhibit in the foyer of Astoria's Maritime Museum. In all the years he owned the Argo, he never replaced the ancient Atlas, convinced the gentle, rhythmic hum of the diesel lured the tuna to his boat. His ability to discern the precise blue of the water indicating the presence of a school of albacore was legendary. His location he always radioed out to other fishermen in the vicinity. They were a loyal fraternity, helping each other find fish.

I think the fraternity of the docks was his refuge from a houseful of women. I surprised him once with a visit to the boat where I thought I would find him laboring away. Instead, he was sitting at the table in the galley with several other boat owners drinking thick, black boat coffee out of heavy white mugs. Boat coffee is grounds tossed directly into boiling water and left to steep. They called it "skookum," a Chinook Indian word for strong. The men were poker-playing, story-swapping veterans of adventures at sea. If you had to be in port, a friendly game of poker and a dash of bourbon in your afternoon coffee would have to do.

My mother leaned on my father to include me in his single-minded fishing life by taking me to work on the boat. I could tell he was not especially enthusiastic about this. He gave me the job of repainting the name on the stern. Nothing is ever still on the water. The dock swayed, the boat rocked, I lurched. I painted the incised lines of the letters as straight as I could. Glossy black paint against the bright white enamel. But the wood was chipped and the dock would float one way, the boat another. I tried to balance and paint. I thought I did a pretty good job, given the conditions. No praise came, but no reproof, either. I don't know if he painted over my work, but it was the only time I was invited to help on the boat. He was a perfectionist.

I think of him as Jason on the Argo, his fellows the Argonauts, searching not for the Golden Fleece but for albacore they traded for gold. He was slender and over six feet tall. My girlfriends in high school would say in a swoony way, "Your father is so-o-o good looking." I was proud to be seen walking through town with him, out on a rare errand together.

In his memoirs, he wrote about schools of albacore so thick you could walk on them. He wrote of Alaskan adventures, outrunning Russian trawlers, facing down armed Caribbean pirates, barely surviving a fire at sea, lobbying in Washington for tariffs on Japanese imports of tuna. When it was nearly finished, my mother looked over his manuscript and saw that he had included a section of photos but none of his three daughters. She was appalled and insisted he include at least one. This was the power of a life on the ocean—a life so absorbing that even in its retelling he forgets his own daughters.

## SLIDING

Winter snow was infrequent in Astoria, so when we had a rare, six-inch snowfall we knew we would go sliding down Seventeenth Street that night. (We called it sliding, not sledding—much less formal.) The course was five steeply descending city blocks, Irving to Duane.

We hauled our Flexi-Flyers out after dinner to the launch site a few blocks away. I can still feel the nervous anticipation of hurtling myself off the edge of Irving Avenue and sliding down that long, steep hill. Parents blocked off each intersection with bonfires so the run would be safe. Safe from cars, at least. Today when I stand at the top and look down Seventeenth Street I can't imagine careening head-first down one of the steepest streets in town. I know my mother worried, but she always let us go. No one was ever hurt.

Truth be told, the snow was usually so wet and heavy we couldn't go very fast and often did not reach Duane five blocks down the hill. We tried to improve our speed by waxing the narrow metal runners. Even in slow snow I wasn't brave enough to go down by myself, so I would find a boy to ride with. It wasn't just the exhilaration of the ride, it was the sixth grade thrill of being so close to a boy. There was little time to savor the pleasurable sensation of layering myself on top of a barely familiar boy before we pushed off. I do remember feeling his muscles flex as we steered the sled by shifting our bodies. Sometimes we would throw ourselves off the sled at the bottom and roll, laughing, embarrassed at the contact, into the piles of snow at the edge of the street.

When it was cold enough and the snow was dry, I was wonderfully terrified at the speed of the run. I hung on to the boy for dear life.

Once the run ended on the flat, there was the long trudge back up the hill. Sometimes a parent would be there with a chained-up pickup to help kids uphill for a few blocks. Being towed on our sled was almost as much fun as sliding down. By the time we climbed back to the top, we had to have yet one more well-earned run.

I can still feel the romance of being allowed out after dark, the exhilarating cold, the warm fires at each intersection, the feel of a bundled-up boy beneath me. Never have I felt so alive.

Maureen and I played together a lot in fourth and fifth grades. She was an only child so we had each other to ourselves when we played at her house. I preferred going there even though we had to be very quiet because her mother was always in bed. She was a mysterious presence in the house. Only once was I invited upstairs to say hello to her mother. The room was light and pleasant, the bed strewn with magazines and books. Her mother wore a pink chenille bed jacket. I was curious to know what was wrong with her. She looked okay to me. Maureen could not say. Maureen was thin and gaunt, with dark circles under her dark eyes. She had a tangled mane of thick, dark hair she couldn't manage well by herself. I don't know how often, if ever, her mother came down from her bedroom to care for Maureen. Later I realized she was essentially motherless.

Maureen's house was more exotic than mine, not just because of her mother but because of all the little jewelry boxes her father brought home from his jewelry store for her to play with. Black velvety boxes lined with white silk or ornate plastic ones decorated with gold. We made entire towns with these boxes.

The other kids thought Maureen was odd, but until fifth grade that didn't bother me. Then I became aware that my friendship with Maureen would probably jeopardize the possibility of my being accepted by the more popular girls. I really, really wanted that.

One day I told Maureen I didn't want to be friends anymore. We were walking up Twelfth Street. She burst into tears, ran across the street and threw herself to the ground in front of a church. I walked on, numb. I felt bad about it for years. I knew I was Maureen's only friend, but I avoided her from then on. Much later, at a twenty-fifth high school reunion, I apologized. She thanked me with such feeling it seemed as though she had needed that apology ever since grade school. Maureen was no longer dark and gaunt. Her face was full and light, she had a good marriage, two children. She looked happy. We cried, we talked, and then we hugged goodbye.

# BAPTISM

Even though my parents were Lutheran, I was baptized as a baby by Bishop Rowe, the traveling Episcopal bishop of southeastern Alaska, whose circuit brought him to Sitka where I was born. I view it as a baptism of some distinction.

But that was not good enough for the small fundamentalist church I attended in high school in Astoria, Oregon. I stopped going with my family to the more mainstream Trinity Lutheran and went instead to the Christian Church. You wouldn't see any prominent citizens of our small town attending this church, and it was not one I would be interested in, except that Bobby, the basketball star, and Evelyn, the head cheerleader and Bobby's girlfriend, went there. Donny, too, and Beverly. Sunday school, morning service, youth group and evening service. A lot of time to hang out with them. A year ahead of me in high school, they were in the best group and I was desperate for friends. I had recently fallen out of favor with the best group in my own class.

I wasn't a member and Sunday morning became more and more uncomfortable as the mournfully seductive hymn was sung at the end of each service: "Softly and tenderly Jesus is calling, calling for you and for me…. Come home, come home…." Almost everyone who attended was a member, so I knew they were waiting and watching for me. I wouldn't go down to the front, I would not, I would not. One morning, to my dismay, I did. Sobbing, I couldn't take the pressure any longer. Immediately I wanted to retrace my steps, but there I was down in front holding the minister's hand. He always seemed like a creepy guy to me, and I usually tried to avoid him. Something about the way he would appear out of nowhere in the basement hallway. Now I was repeating his words, confessing Jesus as my lord and personal savior. The small congregation filed down to greet me with hugs, tears and congratulations. I went home as fast as I could.

Later I was told that I had to be baptized—their way. I told my parents, but I wouldn't let them come to church that Sunday. I had never paid much attention to the big tank in a corner near the altar.

The dreaded Sunday morning came. I undressed in a small room and put on a gown of white sheeting. I entered the sanctuary and waded into the tank where the pastor stood in water up to his knees in his white sheet, waiting for me. I was dunked over backwards and came up dripping, the white sheet clinging to me, almost transparent. His was clinging and almost transparent too. My skin crawled. In my fifteen-year-old mind I thought being baptized this way was really Hicksville. Southern and ignorant. I hated every moment of it. But I had come this far and couldn't see a way out. That was the price I paid to be with my friends.

Occasionally I would be asked to substitute for the regular pianist on Sunday mornings. The congregation was too small to afford an organ. I didn't know any more music suitable for church, so the next time I was asked to play, I adapted a piece I knew for the offering, playing slowly and reverently.

As I was leaving after the service the minister's wife took me aside and said, "Carol, don't ever play that in church again." She knew the music; it was a section from "Slaughter on Tenth Avenue." I was secretly pleased she recognized it. I think it was my way of pushing back in the power struggle for my soul. They had won, temporarily. They had gotten me down to the front of the congregation to confess and they had gotten to dunk me, but I was letting them know I was not one of them. I escaped when I left for college and never went back.

PICO

I was away at college so I didn't get to know Pico, our parakeet, but he and my sister Sharon were best friends. She was a freshman in high school and would take him out of his cage every day after school to play with him. Her idea of play was, for example, to put him in the freezer for a few moments. She couldn't remember for exactly how long. I can imagine his little bird-feet sticking to the frozen metal floor of the freezer, but when I quizzed her she swore they didn't stick.

She would also put him under the kitchen faucet and let the cold water run. I don't believe non-ducks are supposed to be drenched, but she said he didn't seem to suffer any ill effects from this either. I just hope she didn't soak him first and then put him in the freezer.

When she was sick, home from school and bored, she would ask Mother to bring Pico to her bed. She would put him under the sheets, produce a fart and listen to his coughing. I didn't know birds could cough.

Another fun thing she dreamed up for him was to place a claw on one side of a draw drapery and his other claw on the second drapery and slowly pull them apart. I don't think she pulled them very far apart, but she did say this created quite a sense of alarm in the poor bird. Perhaps she was conducting a test of avian memory, since his alarm seemed to suggest she had done this before. If this is reminding you of some medieval torture techniques of the Spanish Inquisition, we're on the same page.

Apparently, she was the only one who paid any attention to Pico, and when she came home from school he would flutter and jump around in his cage and immediately jump onto her finger when she put her hand in his cage. He seemed eager to play, and her intent was not to hurt him but to amuse herself. Apparently, he was amused too.

One of her more ingenious tricks was placing him on the turntable of the record player. There was a fuzzy fabric covering on it so his little claws got stuck in the fabric. He would hang on for dear life as she started the turntable at 33 rpm's and then moved it up to 45, and then . . . 78. He did fall over then and she would pick him up and steady him on his feet.

My sister was born with a quirky sense of humor. With Pico, she pushed the limits of her quirkiness. Sure, she worked our various cats over, dressing them in baby clothes and making them walk in baby shoes, but that was pretty ordinary stuff. Even when she would tease Louie with a morsel of human food like bologna, it was hardly turntable caliber. She would open her hand and snatch it away just in time so he could not get it. Strike one. Snatch it away a second time. Strike two. Snatch it away a third time. Strike three and you're out. Ha ha. She was just amusing herself. But a bird stuck on a turntable was quite a few notches above teasing a cat. I'm sure she didn't mean to harm Pico and would have been horrified if she had. At the same time, she was very careful not to let Mother know what she was doing.

We thought Pico was a boy until one day we found two small eggs on the floor of his cage at Christmas. Perhaps all that stimulating activity inspired Pico to become her own creative self. Did she lay them in gratitude for all the fun or in self-defense, as in "I'll be a mom soon and will have better things to do than to let you play with me." The eggs were not fertile; probably a good thing, if you know what I mean.

As a young child, my sister Sharon was afraid of black airplanes and insisted the closet door in her bedroom be firmly shut before she could go to sleep. We laughed about these fears. No one knew what black airplanes were. A child's imagination.

It was only recently I realized where her fear of black airplanes came from. On occasional Saturday evenings when my parents and guests were suitably inebriated, my father would entertain them by putting my three-year-old sister into a piece of black luggage, snap it shut and swing her round and round. He would then let her out and she would stagger around the room, to the hilarity of the guests. She was happy to entertain everyone and be the center of attention. Her fear of black airplanes was the price she paid for their attention. I can only imagine the claustrophobia she must have felt. The black suitcase was usually stored in the closet in her room. In her child's imagination it might escape from the closet and get her in her sleep if the door were left open.

Sharon resisted staying in her crib at night, so my parents would tie her in. She became adept at picking knots. On party evenings, she was given permission to untie herself to escape. My father would tie a diaper around her ankle and attach it to her crib with as tight a knot as he could tie and then time her to see how long it took her to pick the knot, climb out of the crib, and run to the living room to the applause of the guests. The family Houdini.

Tethering a child to her crib or using a child for adult amusement is, to put it gently, misguided. Might this have been the seeds of her wicked sense of humor; her questionable "play" with Pico, the parakeet; her taunting of old Mr. Jaffee, an itinerant gardener from Israel?

Sharon told me that while Mother braided her hair she would flinch if she pulled too hard and Mother would slap her cheek to make her sit still. One day Mother noticed Sharon flinched even before the braiding had begun. To her credit, she recognized how unaware she had been of her automatic slapping and burst into tears. She stopped the slapping.

My friend Janice lived just up the street, but I didn't like to play at her house. When her mother was mad at her, which was most of the time, she would pull Janice's hair hard and make her cry. Janice was afraid of her mother, and I was too.

I drew my own line in the sand against corporal punishment when I was about nine and sitting at the kitchen table with my father. I was kicking the crossbar absent-mindedly as I was eating my sandwich. My father asked me to stop several times and I ignored him. He lost his temper and said, "Ok, to the basement for a spanking." I went down with him, and before he could raise his hand I began to scream as loudly and as long as I could. It was a wonderful wail. I had noted my advantage on the way down. The windows were wide open so our very close next door neighbors would hear my wailing. My father never started the spanking. I don't think his heart was in it anyway, and I believe we both knew that at nine I was too old for spankings.

## The Farm

My grandfather built everything on his farm in Poulsbo, near Seattle. I imagine it looked very much like the small farms of his native Norway, with buildings of unpainted vertical wood siding. My mother would take us there every summer for several weeks and again at Thanksgiving. I didn't like going to the farm as a child. The ride was long and tedious. There was no use protesting. It was where she grew up. She loved being with her mother, her sister and her two nieces. Sometimes her other sister would be visiting from Wisconsin with her two daughters.

In spite of grumbling about those visits to the farm, today they are among my treasured memories. As a kid, I didn't appreciate the mythical, magical place it was. Until we got there, that is, and set out to explore and re-explore every inch of it. My grandfather was a carpenter who built his farm from scratch, as early pioneers did. He logged the fir trees, built a sawmill to mill the trees, and built his house and all the outbuildings. Besides the three-bedroom main house, there was a large barn, a one-room cabin, a garage, a wash house, an outhouse, a woodshed, a smoke house, a chicken house, a pig sty, and a picket fence. Except for the farmhouse and cabin, the outbuildings were unpainted. The picket fence enclosed the people buildings and the apple orchard. The animal buildings were beyond the fence. Over the years the bare wood of the outbuildings has mellowed into a beautiful silver gray, contrasting with the dark fir forest surrounding the homestead. I think the farm should be on the National Register of Historic Places. My grandparents are considered pioneer founders of the small Norwegian settlement an hour by ferry across Puget Sound from Seattle. Poulsbo was originally "Paul's Place," named for Paul Wahl who arrived in the 1880s and set up a logging camp. When the post office was established there, the name was misspelled and the town became Poulsbo. Today it is a summer retreat for Seattleites and boasts a large yacht harbor. This is the fate of "discovered" towns—gentrified this time with a harbor full of sleek sailboats across Main Street from feed stores, lumber yards and hardware stores serving the real business of this farm community.

After the long road trip and a perfunctory greeting to the family, we would set out to explore. My grandfather's cobbler shop was especially interesting, with its iron soles shaped like feet used to repair shoes, and my grandmother's wash house with its several sizes of irons which she would heat on the huge cast iron wood stove. There was no electricity or running water until I was in high school. I felt useful and important when I was asked to get a bucket of water. I didn't mind walking down the sloping yard past the apple orchard to pump a bucketful, but carrying it back up was a heavy task.

We avoided the mysterious cabin which my grandfather had built for Uncle Alvin who had died there of tuberculosis. We never went into the cabin, just peeked in the windows. It was kept as a shrine to the unknown Uncle Alvin. We cousins scared each other saying that he might still be in there, languishing. The bed in which he died was still there, stripped down to its iron springs. Uncle Alvin was my aunt's first husband, who died before any of us were born. This lent her a special mystique, mostly because nobody would talk about him and because she was married to her second husband. It occurs to me now how heartbreaking this must have been. Signa, young, in love and married, moving to the big city, Seattle. Her handsome young husband gets sick. She brings him back to the farm where her father builds a special little cabin just for them. Signa was his first child. How he must have loved her and ached for her heartbreak.

Later Aunt Signa married a man who courted her by swatting her across her rear end with a salmon he had just caught. She worked at a soda fountain in Poulsbo and was leaning over scooping ice cream when the romantic inspiration came to him. She married him anyway. His family had developed a mink business in Alaska, but World War I interfered and people were not buying mink coats. So they shipped the skins home and the family was overdressed in unsold mink for years. But I don't think that was why she married him. I think it was for his sense of humor.

My grandfather worked in town building houses and was the proud owner of two vehicles, one an early version of a pickup and the other a Ford Model A, both black, of course. That was the only available color in the first Fords. We were not allowed to play around the car unless my grandfather was there. Unlike our own car, it had a high running board, isinglass windows, and a windup crank starter. This vehicle was as breathlessly exotic as if I were taking a ride in a spaceship today. As subsistence farmers, they did it all themselves—built their own shelter, raised their own food, repaired their own vehicles. When they had sheep my grandmother would card, spin and knit her long, wool under slips on needles so fine the finished garment was not at all bulky.

I remember my grandmother reading the newspaper with a magnifying glass in the dim light of a kerosene lamp. I occasionally use her magnifying glass today. For us kids, bedtime was a dreaded time, partly because we would be herded upstairs soon after sunset and partly because I knew we would have to use the chamber pot in the morning. I don't know why we didn't go to the outhouse first thing, but we never did. I imagined the mess if I tipped the pot over. I never did. Just as disagreeable, though, was the outhouse, with its hold-your-nose odor, buzzing flies, occasional bee, resident spiders and newspapers for toilet paper. I would put off a trip to the outhouse as long as I could.

Aside from having to use the chamber pot, mornings were the best time of day. My grandmother would rise before dawn and make potato bread for us using the sweet, creamy potatoes my grandfather cultivated. We raced from our lazy beds to be the first to get a hot setacacca fresh out of the oven—a Norwegian English muffin, only better—which we loaded with homemade blackberry jam. To this day I prefer bread over any dessert. You might notice I omitted the butter. Both the butter and milk had a strong taste, depending on what the cows had eaten recently, not like the consistent, bland taste of the pasteurized milk and butter we were used to from the market. My sisters and I would refuse my grandmother's milk and butter, shunning the humble but precious offering.

When it rained we played in the big bedroom upstairs. One day I discovered a tiny gold key in a drawer. I didn't tell anyone, my secret prize. I searched for its lock but found none. This was a project that occupied me for several afternoons, looking through closets and cabinets. Then I lost the key. I went over every inch of the big bedroom on my knees. I never found the key, which became even more precious lost. But the bare wood floor is equally precious in my memory, with its distinct grain. I came to know every inch of that floor, looking for my lost gold key. I can still see the work of my grandfather's plane.

Sometimes my mother's two sisters would be there with their children. Seven girl cousins. I remember the women sitting at the big round kitchen table with Grandma, drinking coffee, laughing, and telling stories. In Norwegian. We knew they were talking about us, which was both flattering because they were enjoying themselves so much and frustrating because we were excluded from these entertaining stories. We would hang around their chairs, pestering them, hoping they would switch to English. They would just shoo us away.

There was a stand of trees a short walk beyond the front gate which we called the park. We spent the hot summer days in the coolness under the tall trees, fashioning crowns, bracelets, and even skirts out of tough, leathery salal leaves which we would stitch together with twigs. We were the princesses of the forest. In the evenings, the adults would sometimes take us through the park and along the dark, narrow path to Mrs. Winter's house for a visit. Mrs. Winter served thick sour cream topped with cinnamon and sugar to the ladies—a Norwegian crème fraiche. We were assured we would not like its tart taste. I was convinced and don't think I ever tasted it. Later I realized it was too precious to share with children.

When we were in dire need of candy, we would walk the mile to the store at the crossroads. That's a long way for a kid to walk for candy on a hot July day on a dusty road. Auntie Inga's chocolate cake was good, but sooner or later it couldn't stand up to our need for NECCO wafers, a Big Hunk, or a Milky Way. So we would trudge to the store over the unpaved, dusty Nelson Road, named for our grandfather, hoping no car would come along and choke us with the brown dust. When candy was two for a penny or a penny, a dime each would buy enough to last the long walk back.

My grandfather's name was changed when he was processed through Ellis Island. Agent: What's your name? GF: Hans Stenodegaard. Agent: What is your father's name? GF: Nels Stenodegaard. Agent: Your name's Nelson. Next.

My grandmother spoke very little English, so I really didn't know her. By the time I was ten, she was almost eighty, bent over, toothless, dressed in shapeless dresses, every bit the woman from the Old Country. I was afraid of her, and my mother told me she didn't like to hold little children, so I probably never sat on her lap. I did sit on my grandfather's lap and became very fond of him, following him around the farm. He looks proud in the snapshot of three-year-old me with him at the stone wheel out by the woodshed where he sharpened his scythes.

My grandmother was born in 1869 and emigrated from Norway in her early thirties. She married in 1905, and her daughters were born when she was thirty-six, forty and forty-four, ages at which people were more likely to die than to give birth. Since she got a late start, it's a good thing she lived to be ninety-seven. It has been said that the pain of permanent family separation takes three generations to heal. Grandmother and daughter feel it; granddaughter hears about it. My grandmother refused to speak of her voyage in steerage, her refusal eloquent and firm. My imagining is more vivid than if she had described it. Steerage is the space between decks for poor passengers. Crowded, poorly lit, smelly, dangerous. Passengers seasick. She had with her only a basket and a very small trunk on which she sat during the long voyage. Did she have a bunk for sleeping or was her trunk her only space? My sister has restored her trunk, painting the embossed metal skin a glossy pink, black, and white, as if to seal in the pain.

The closets on the farm were mostly empty. My grandfather had three changes of clothing at the most. My grandmother the same. One day I was snooping and, in the dark at the very back of her closet, where the ceiling slanted under the staircase, I found a beautiful black lace cape adorned with jet beads. A ruffled collar. Impossibly romantic to my eyes. This cape was a peek into my grandmother's sensuality, with its flirty allure. My grandmother, wizened and bent from age and unremitting hard work, had been a handsome woman who wore something of beauty when she was young. I was happy to see that she had in her life an object of pleasure and pride. Where would she wear something so exotic? To church, of course. The small white Lutheran church with the traditional soaring bell tower is on a hill with a view of the harbor, one block above Poulsbo's main street. My grandparents are buried there in the church cemetery. My cousin informs me there is still an unclaimed space in the family plot. I plan to be buried there in the company of my stoic grandparents and make peace with the invading sailboats in the harbor.

The family of five consumed most of the vegetables, butter, eggs, and milk produced on the farm. Carrots and potatoes would be stored for the winter in the cool but creepy dirt cellar. I ventured down there only when I was asked to bring up vegetables for supper. It's the fastest chore I ever did as a child.

Occasionally my grandmother would invite one of us girls to help her gather eggs. We would tiptoe into the henhouse so as not to disturb the chickens. I never quite got the knack of slipping my hand under a warm chicken and stealing her egg without being pecked, but my mother could. I watched my mother's concentration as she milked the cows or chopped wood. I could see how much she enjoyed these tasks. We kids always wanted to jump in the hay in the barn. This we were not allowed to do because jumping in it knocked the nutritious heads off the top of the stalks. We begged to sleep overnight in the hay. The aunts relented once. It was dusty, itchy and awful. We lasted about an hour before we came back to the house, defeated. It had seemed like such a good idea. At haying time, we waited at the house until the borrowed horses returned with the big wooden wagon stacked high with hay. Then we were allowed to jump on it for the short ride to the barn.

In spite of what might sound like bounty, my mother told me she was sometimes hungry. Often the only meat they had for dinner were a few small cubes of salt pork with their potatoes. My mother lost some of her teeth early in life. An orange in the toe of the Christmas stocking was a miraculous treat. She admitted she would not have been able to walk the miles to high school if her older sister had not gone to work to help pay for her shoes. I ache for their poverty. Yet the demands and richness of this simple life gave my mother strength and determination, which have been her biggest gifts to me.

Today my cousin and her husband live on the farm. They have maintained it as it was and have welcomed any of us who have wanted to visit. I am disappointed to find the road to the farm has been changed from Nelson Road to Noll Road N.E. Who was Noll and why did he supplant Nelson? And why the need for N.E.? Poulsbo is no longer a small farming community. It's large enough to require directional quadrants. Some of my history has been erased.

I feel nostalgic about the farm. My grandparents, mother, and aunts are all gone. I'm now the oldest in my family. The trees have grown thick and tall in the hundred years since my grandfather built the place, and the acreage now has abundant, valuable timber. No one has mentioned selling the farm, but I wonder if there is a conflict between the allure of gain and the preservation of history and home. I'm glad that decision is not mine.

One of my most vivid memories of college is the morning Barbara asked me why I had given her my hot water bottle the night before. I what?! She told me I had met her in the hall on the second floor of the sorority house and tried to give her my red rubber hot water bottle. She declined to take it, and I suppose I went back upstairs to bed. We laughed, both puzzled. I had no idea what she was talking about. Then I realized I must have been sleepwalking.

I had heard of sleepwalking. It was one of those exotic curiosities like tsunamis I had seen depicted in Japanese woodblock prints, not sure if they were fact or fiction. Now I knew it for fact. I was a somnambulist. I was thrilled.

I slept in a top bunk on the third floor sleeping porch. Deeply asleep, I had climbed out of the upper bunk, found my hot water bottle in the bedding and walked out of the sleeping porch and down the stairs to the second floor. I suppose Barbara was the first person I encountered on whom to bestow the gift of my hot water bottle. She had been studying late. The sleeping porch was uninsulated and freezing cold in winter, so we all had thick comforters and slept with hot water bottles. The porch was not wired for electric blankets.

The National Sleep Foundation calls the seemingly simple act of walking a complex behavior, let alone walking in your sleep. I call lowering myself out of an upper bunk in the dark and walking down a flight of stairs all while sound asleep even more complex behavior.

Sleepwalking is thought to occur more commonly when a person is sleep-deprived. Well, that explains everything. When else is a person more sleep-deprived than in college?

Sleepwalking can be hereditary. I hope my father never did it aboard his boat far out in the Pacific Ocean. Sleep experts say that symptoms of sleepwalking behavior range from simply sitting up in bed and looking around, to walking around the room or house, to leaving the house and even driving long distances. It is a common misconception that a sleepwalker should not be awakened. In fact, it can be quite dangerous not to wake a sleepwalker. Hmm, I wonder what happens when a sleepwalker awakens while driving on the freeway.

I loved the idea I had sleepwalked. I had done something rare and unusual, something which distinguished me. Only one to fifteen percent of the population is thought to sleepwalk. I'll claim it, even though I was asleep when I did it. I'm intrigued by the idea that there are parts of me over which I have little or no control. I feel relieved of the big, lonely responsibility of running my life. It's as though I have a creative, adventurous assistant who loves adventure as much as I do. I've never sleepwalked since, that I'm aware of.

I recently spent a few days at my niece's condo in Gearhart, a quiet beach town on the northern Oregon coast. Hers is 1960s motel-style with a view of the ocean, but in the 1920s well-to-do Portlanders claimed a choice stretch of beachfront and built what are now million-dollar summer homes on a lane which came to be known as Gin Ridge, so named for the daily late afternoon rituals performed by its happy summer residents. Most of the grey-shingled homes have been passed down to their grandchildren who continue to extend their tight social scene from Portland Heights to Gearhart for the summer.

If you don't own a home in Gearhart there is little reason to go there. There is one main street from the highway into the tiny town center, and if you aren't watching, you could miss it, which is just fine with the residents of this cozy community. It is murmured they might even have influenced the highway department to omit a sign. Gearhart has that in common with Bolinas, a bohemian California coastal town famous for removing any identifying highway signs.

Gearhart has no glitz like some beach towns. No caramel corn, Ferris wheel, penny arcade. Not even basic goods and services like a hardware store, coin laundry or gas station. There is an ice cream shop, one small restaurant and two realties. The atmosphere of exclusivity is so palpable I felt I needed proof of residence, although being blond helped camouflage my nonresident status.

Gearhart is an irritant to the residents of nearby small towns—the grain of sand in the oyster of that stretch of the Oregon coast. Seaside, Warrenton, Hammond and Astoria are proud working class towns, and most people could not afford second homes, let alone the grand homes of Gearhart. So they ignore it. I grew up about ten miles from Gearhart. As kids we thought it was boring and always bypassed it for the more exciting carnival-like town of Seaside or Cannon Beach. But when I got a job at the Gearhart Hotel for the summer after my freshman year at University of Oregon, I was pleased. I was hired as a waitress, based on my previous experience serving cherry Cokes and hot fudge sundaes in high school at a soda fountain popular with kids. This was not a coveted job. The creepy owner would brush our behinds as we bent over to scoop ice cream. The owner's wife would sit at the end of the counter smoking, glowering at us to make sure we didn't help ourselves to any of the ice cream or a Coke.

The hotel paid minimum wage but provided room and board. I worked the breakfast shift from seven to eleven and buffet dinner from six to nine. The afternoons were mine. It wasn't hard work for a nineteen-year-old, and I had energy to spare to go to the piano bar after my dinner shift to meet my sorority sisters from Portland. Their parents owned homes on Gin Ridge, and Chita and Patty and Lee would have been out all day playing golf or tennis or bridge while I worked, but we were all just friends at the piano bar in the evening. I don't remember feeling inferior or out of place in the black skirt and white blouse of my server's uniform. Somehow, I had made it into a sorority which pledged girls from some of the wealthiest families in the state. I was from a blue-collar family, and I was very interested in this new-to-me wealthy lifestyle.

Two other college students from Minnesota and I were housed in the large unfinished attic of the Ocean House, a much smaller hotel at one end of Gin Ridge and walking distance to the Gearhart Hotel. At night I would add up my tips—all coins, no bills—and fall asleep to the soothing rhythm of the ocean.

In my afternoons off I flirted with Jim Barnes, the lifeguard at the pool, as I worked on my tan and he watched the swimmers—and me, I hoped. It was a romantic summer with Jim. We spent most of our time off together, but the romance did not last past the summer when we both returned to school. Many years later I learned he had had a distinguished career in the Air Force, achieving the rank of colonel, and had taken his own life when he learned he had early Alzheimer's. Elisabeth Kubler-Ross has said there's a special place in heaven for the consolation and care of suicides. Rest in peace, Jim Barnes, with your faculties intact.

Every old hotel has its resident eccentric. The Gearhart had its would-be murderer. My boss warned me more than once to stay away from the boiler room. I couldn't think why I would want to go there anyway, when I had the beach, the pool, my own corner of the Ocean House attic and my friends at the piano bar. I had heard the dark rumors that crazy

"Hatchet Harry" slept on the warm floor of the boiler room. He had earned the name because he had threatened his mother with a hatchet. He was descended from one of Astoria's founding families in the 1800s but one whose genetics and family home had both deteriorated. I saw him once at the hotel. I felt a shudder. I wondered if he still had his hatchet.

I also quaked my first week sending breakfast orders to the cooks, Mark and Marie, whose reputation, especially Marie's, was to give the new waitresses as hard a time as possible. She was skilled at sending threatening, contemptuous looks. I think it was her way of having some fun, tormenting the new waitresses, but she meant to scare them too. Marie had a hard job and wasn't about to tolerate a silly college girl messing up her beautiful breakfast omelets, waffles, or eggs-over-easy. And I wasn't going to let a tough woman from Portland's black ghetto intimidate me, even though I was more afraid of her than of Hatchet Harry. I resolved to meet strength with strength, competence with competence. I got the orders right and I was fast. I wouldn't let her withering looks rattle me. It took several weeks, but when I didn't screw up she reluctantly began to give me the glinty eye of approval. Before the end of the summer we became good working buddies. Marie's respect was not easily won, but I did it. I count that one of my major accomplishments from that time in my life. My parents had given me a strong work ethic which I could match with someone like Marie any day.

That was my best summer. It was the first time I was without adult supervision. Marie didn't frighten me out of a job. Jim the lifeguard was my first college boyfriend. A lifeguard! The stuff of teen romance novels. Even though I had been away at college, the school saw itself as "in loco parentis," in place of the parent. Our hours and whereabouts were carefully controlled and monitored. That summer I was fully responsible for myself. No one was watching me. And I was only ten miles from home if I needed anything. My life was my own and I loved it. Not since have I felt so light, so free, so happy.

## THE PARTY CRASHER

I was two years out of college living on my own in Portland and home for a few days at Christmas when I crashed Sue's Christmas party. Her family was the tacitly acknowledged pinnacle of Astoria society. Her mother's maiden name was the same as a lovely beach town a few miles away. Her mother had a *noblesse oblige* manner; so did Sue. Her father was successful in business as president of a major seafood company. This was not an insignificant party to crash.

When I heard that Sue was having a reunion party for college friends and that I had not been invited, I allowed myself to be hurt for about a minute. Then I shifted gears. I rationalized that she had forgotten to invite me. I had known her since first grade and gone all through school with her. I had attended the same university, had pledged a good sorority. If she had not invited me, I would invite myself.

Fortunately, I had an escort; otherwise, I could not have done it. I had invited Patrick, whom I had been dating in Portland, to spend Christmas with my family, and we had driven from Portland together. Patrick would be my armor against any unpleasant innuendos at the party. He was tall, courtly, handsome, well-dressed, and drove a sporty white Buick with flaring fins.

I timed our arrival carefully. Everyone was already there. This was good—no awkward silences. I smirked inwardly when Sue opened the door, started, recovered herself, and greeted us warmly. *Noblesse oblige*, all right. But I, too, could act.

When I saw how few people were there—only eight or nine—I quickly realized this was not such a good idea. But I stayed in role—the happy-to-be-there invited guest. The loveseat was vacant; Patrick and I sat. Desperate for something to talk about, we commented to Sue's mother how comfortable, how beautiful it was, with its yellow and white silk brocade upholstery and fine down cushions. I knew good stuff when I saw it. I was an equal but a very uneasy one.

We were merry and talkative—*lovely party, delicious eggnog*. We didn't stay long. Wished everyone a merry Christmas and said goodbye.

Of course, I've wondered why I was not invited. I believe it had to do with a conflict between my father and Sue's father. My father had met with him as a representative of the fishermen to negotiate fairer prices. Labor and management. Prior to that meeting they had been friendly, respected each other. This time her father would not budge. My father was not prone to losing his temper, but he would not tolerate perceived injustice. I had heard that my father may have accused and insulted him about how he was treating the fishermen, not paying them fairly, perhaps even cheating them.

The automatic, unreflecting way in which I went about planning to crash Sue's party has always puzzled me. It was as though I were obeying some imperative. I now know I was. The power of the unconscious continues to astound me. Unwittingly, I was evening the score for my father: President Tom, 1; Fish Producer Fred, 1.

Sue and I have never talked about my crashing her party. Over the years when we have occasionally crossed paths she has greeted me warmly and, occasionally, with frosty undertones.

The idea for a money memoir was suggested in *Emotional Currency*, by Kate Levinson, to help women with their often problematic relationship to money.

Well, that was me all over when I thought about it. I've never felt I had enough even when I had enough. Some mornings I think about what will get me out of bed and often it's about money—checking my bank balance, Visa bill, IRA, my budget.

I'm aware I mention money too frequently. I ask what others pay. I mention a large purchase I have just made and am irked when no one asks how much I paid. They deprive me of discussing my tendency to be extravagant.

I feel resentful of what others have or seem to have, especially here in the Bay Area. Even though I like my small condo, I wish I had a bigger one or a house. I notice others' jewelry, cars, houses, furniture.

Worrying about money must go way back, as most persistent problems do. When I was five I got a nickel allowance and Mother and I would go to Newberry's dime store to spend it. No problem there, only minor angst in having to choose only one toy.

When my father was in port he came home from the boat every evening and would head down the hall to the bathroom for a bath. He would hang his pants on a hook on the bathroom door where they would stay until morning. I began to take money from his pocket. I was about eight years old. Pennies and nickels at first. As I got bolder I moved up to dimes and quarters. It was so easy. I added taking money from my mother's wallet which she kept in her purse on a shelf in the living room coat closet. This was trickier because the coat closet was right around the corner from the kitchen where my mother would be preparing dinner. There was no reason for me to go into the coat closet, so I had to wait until my mother was busy at the sink when she would have her back to me.

If they knew I was taking money they did not let on right away. One day I was on the boat with my father and found a cigar box full of his poker money. I helped myself. He must have seen me. On the way home he said, very gently, very lovingly, "You'd better not take any more money out of the cigar box, Carol." I was stung. I felt so ashamed to have my father know what a little thief I was. His esteem was worth more to me than oxygen. I never did it again.

I would sometimes hear my parents in hushed, serious conversations in the breakfast nook. I imagined they were discussing money. We children would be barred from the kitchen during these meetings.

I would see my father laboring over his income taxes, balls of crumpled paper all around him on the floor.

In the sixth grade I stole lipstick from Gunderson's dime store. I even shoplifted from Cost Plus into my twenties until one day I decided that it was risky and foolish and stopped, partly because of moral and legal considerations and partly because I had decided I could not compete with my friends who also stole from Cost Plus. G. and R. would fill a huge straw laundry basket with dishes, bedspreads and artwork and pay only for the basket. They would later brag about their swag. The cashier was a friend. I couldn't keep up with them.

Cost Plus was our Anthropologie. Every Saturday it drew my roommates and me like a magnet, dazzled we were by the array of Indian bedspreads, imported glassware, hanging papasan chairs, Mexican hammocks, exquisitely embroidered blouses, rattan and wicker furniture, and assorted boxes covered in shiny red and orange or blue and green paper. We would stagger home with armloads of stuff to decorate our apartment. I wouldn't dream of shoplifting when I was with them.

In high school I felt deprived with only two cashmere sweaters, one of which I paid for myself with my babysitting money. My other sweaters were the less expensive "Wondermeres," a blend of wool and rabbit fur. Naturally I compared myself to the girls who had more cashmeres, not to the ones who had none.

I was confused when I saw the amount of my father's yearly income on a scholarship application for college. How could such a small amount send me to college? I had nothing on which to base my appraisal, but it seems the university agreed we needed financial help and I was awarded a small tuition scholarship.

After I "dropped out" about 1969 and friends were working in corporate jobs, moving up, buying beautiful clothes and cars, traveling, and buying homes, some days I had to decide whether to use a stamp or deliver a PG&E payment in person. For a person who felt she never had enough, I lived comfortably for some years on very little. Hoping to improve my situation, I applied for a corporate job but by then my resume had a few holes in it, and I was not considered.

Many of my women friends have an ex-husband or two in their history, and the proceeds of those marriages have set them up nicely. I've made every penny on my own, except for a small payout from a profit-sharing plan at a law firm where I worked and a modest inheritance from my mother. When I am at my most petty I think how much easier it would have been if I had had a divorce settlement. When I'm into resentment, I don't think about the huge emotional cost of a divorce. It's not free money.

Perhaps stemming from my college experience, I am attracted to people with money. One friend has a lot of it. It can be freeing to be around someone who doesn't give money a second thought. Except that can go awry. Sometimes her credit charges won't go through because her card is maxed out. It's been said that you always know when a person has money— they never have any. A client once told me, "We're rich but we're not wealthy." A wealth manager told me the demarcation figure is about ten million. When I've traveled with a well-to-do friend, I've made expensive, impulsive jewelry purchases. On Mykonos for fun we went into the best jewelry shop. I bought a gold necklace and earrings from a shop which has branches only in Paris, Tokyo, Geneva and New York. I think I did it to compete with and impress her. How foolish was that? Turns out it has quadrupled in value.

Essentially, I was like the ant and the grasshopper. My twenties and thirties were my grasshopper years. My friends say I retired first and went to work later. I didn't begin to make any money until after the age of fifty, so I didn't have much time to catch up. My financial life has mirrored the instability of the rest of my life. I don't have a quarrel with the rest of my life now, but I still sometimes quarrel with money. Some days I am stingy with myself. Other days I become exasperated with imagined scarcity and spend. What works for me when I want to save and spend at the same time is to buy something expensive, keep it for a few days and then return it. One family member has married a high-earner and they are reaping handsome rewards—cars, trips, houses. She has come to expect abundance. One of my sisters, on the other hand, has very little. She eats well but frugally and drinks weak coffee. Some of her kitchen gadgets are old enough, and dull enough, to be sold in antique shops. Yet she doesn't seem to stress about money at all. I marvel. She is an old soul.

I don't like this perpetual feeling of not having enough, this feeling that others are much better off, and I'm trying to keep up. When I joined the most prestigious athletic/social club in Portland for a hefty buy-in, I was critical of what I thought was the self-satisfied look on the faces of other members.

I suspect there are as many words for money as there are for dying. I suspect ninety-nine percent of advertisements are about money. I suspect many other people feel they don't have enough either.

I make lists of what I would do for my family if I won a very large lottery. I'd pay off everyone's mortgage, buy everyone a new car, take them all on a grand trip. I'd be patron to a young artist. Winning would force me to decide what difference I could make on the environment, peace, hunger, health. I would be a philanthropist, but only after I have "enough."

These conflicts about money are obviously about self-worth, not financial worth. My self-worth is connected more to doing productive, worthwhile work than it is to an abstract dollar figure. What a long way around to a simple truth.

I've always been a late bloomer.

# BEING THERE
# (Detour into the Sixties)

I finished college at University of Oregon with a bachelor's in European history. What then? I was twenty-two. I remember feeling poised on the edge of something, waiting for something to happen. I was not worried, just waiting. Most of my college friends were planning weddings. I didn't even have a boyfriend. When Christy asked me to share an apartment in Portland with her and Gail, I was so relieved to have somewhere to go I ignored the obvious—that she and Gail were both engaged and would be moving out in a few months to get married. She invited me to share a place so she could pay less rent. We were not close. Christy had chosen the apartment without consulting Gail or me. I think she chose badly. It was way out on the east side. To me it was the wrong side of town. What did she know? She was from Southern California.

We lived there for the summer. When I realized that working forty hours a week in a go-nowhere, boring job was much harder than taking eighteen hours in college, I distracted myself by reading *Lady Chatterley's Lover*, newly available. After work I would retreat to my bedroom if it was not my turn to cook, then stagger out after an hour of reading, drunk with vicarious passion and sex, amazed I could have such a book in my hands.

When it was my turn to cook, I decided to grill on a hibachi in the kitchen with the one window open wide; we didn't have a patio or a deck. When the starter ignited the briquettes too quickly, smoke poured out the open window. I tended the hibachi, knowing it was all under control. The neighbors didn't and called the fire department. Engines arrived and we had to endure stern lessons on hibachi cooking. A scolding was fine. I had feared arrest.

Christy had been the Sweetheart of Sigma Chi. I think that gave her ideas of glamour. One day she brought home an elderly MG sports car. Like Christy, it looked good on the outside but did not run well on the inside. Every morning for at least fifteen minutes she had to rev the hell out of the engine so it wouldn't die on her way to work. At seven a.m. the roaring, farting, barking noise reverberated throughout the apartment complex. I'm surprised the neighbors didn't call the police over this disturbance. I considered it myself.

Three months after settling in, my roommates moved out to be married. I was left holding the bag in the form of the year lease we had signed. I guess none of us thought a year really meant a year. We didn't have money to pay off the lease. I assumed I had to bear full responsibility for it, since I couldn't use the marriage excuse. The landlord allowed me to move to a cheaper place he owned on the west side where I lived out the lease. The "better" west side, but not a better apartment. In the 1920s that studio had been a gem, with its brownish pink paint and its 1920s state-of-the-art appliances. Unchanged forty years later, it was a dark and dingy hole. Today the owner's name is attached to many civic and philanthropic projects in Portland. I think "slum landlord" when I see his name.

My unmarried college friends had been struggling through a grueling first year teaching high school. Then they left town for summer school in Hawaii. Abandoned once again, I decided to become a teacher so I too could go to Hawaii for the summer. I was working forty hours a week during the day, and four nights a week I took classes toward a teaching credential at the local college. My alma mater didn't tell me a major in European history would not qualify me to teach high school. So I earned the equivalent of a second bachelor's in English. For those two years, Hawaii beckoned just over the horizon. I moved to Eugene for the required two quarters of student teaching where I was assigned sophomore English and . . . world history. Later it occurred to me that world history might just include European history, but I was so frightened by student teaching that the irony of this was lost on me.

We began with the ancient world. I thought I needed to know the entire history of Greece and Rome to teach high school sophomores. I tore through Will and Ariel Durant's thousand pages of *The Life of Greece* (volume two of eleven volumes of *The Story of Civilization*) and *Caesar and Christ* (volume three). I began to realize maybe I didn't have to know the entire history of the ancient world and that, compared to me, my students knew almost nothing. I relaxed, slightly. The English class was worse. My master teacher asked me to devise a multiple-choice test. I worked most of the night on it. When she rejected the entire thing, I knew I would quit. I spent the remainder of the quarter reading aloud to the students as if they were in kindergarten. This could not in any way be deemed teaching English to sophomores.

Wanting summers off is not a strong enough incentive to go through what it takes to become a teacher. I didn't sign up for the required second quarter. I've only been a little bit sorry. I never did learn how to design a multiple-choice test. Much later in my graduate psychology program I learned that designing a good one is fiendishly difficult.

After student teaching I got a job in the admissions office at the University of Oregon. That was a juicy spot. In my spare time I could look up the grades of everyone I had known in college.

One Saturday, sorority sister Jean came to see me in Eugene. She was one of the teachers who had gone to Hawaii but had decided that two years teaching high school English was enough. Casually she asked if I wanted to move to San Francisco. What an easy question. No multiple choice there. A month later and a day after my sister's June wedding, we drove Jean's old blue and white Chevy down a sweltering I-5 to San Francisco. We had an apartment waiting for us in Pacific Heights. I had an introduction to an attorney where I was immediately offered a job at a prestigious law firm.

I bought a dress to wear to work, a rich whipping cream color, smooth fabric, all cotton. It had a stiff, two-inch wide belt which meant I had to sit at my typewriter as stiffly as the belt. I wore a panty girdle encasing my thighs to keep everything from jiggling. I hardly dared breathe. The dress wrinkled anyway. For five years I worked trussed up like this, first at the law firm and then at a management consulting firm on Montgomery Street. The attorneys at the law firm and the management consultants, all men, were from the same prestigious schools—Harvard, Stanford, Michigan. The young attorneys were so self-important they didn't even greet us secretaries with a morning hello. At the management consulting firm, a secretary came in wearing one of the first miniskirts. She was sent home in disgrace to change her clothes. This was 1966, and I was still an obedient product of the fifties. But rebellion was simmering.

One early morning it was my turn to deliver coffee to the men one floor down at the management consulting firm. I had been delayed on the phone by my manager in Los Angeles. When I arrived with the coffee one of the men said, "Well, it's about time!" I retorted without thinking, "You're sure a picky bastard." I heard soft, warning mutterings as I left. In the time it took me to go up one floor, I lost control. I closed myself in an empty office and began to sob. Someone found me, but I couldn't stop crying. I went home. I made some martinis. I drank them. When I walked down the hall to the bathroom I fell flat on my face. For the rest of the day I slept on the sofa. No one said anything about the bruise on my face at work the next day. Soon after, I was demoted from office manager to somebody's secretary. Then I quit.

I had stepped out of line and there were serious consequences. Women at that time did not assert, let alone talk back. It was before assertiveness training became popular. Certainly, I was mouthy and insulting to the guy. I didn't realize how much I had been suppressing—how angry I was with my micromanaging boss, the privileged professionals, the insignificance of my job, and, above all, the implied insignificance of me. I had been trying to make myself more valuable by working long hours. Sometimes I wouldn't catch a bus home before 8:30 at night.

I had done well in college and was now a typist. Before I graduated it didn't occur to me to line up to meet recruiters who came to campus. They came to recruit the guys. Newspaper classifieds read "Help Wanted Men" or "Help Wanted Women." That's just the way it was. I was steeped in the distinction and at the same time angry about it. There were four jobs open to women at the time—wife and mother, nurse, teacher or secretary. I think now I was so thoroughly conditioned by these limitations that I needed to make trouble for myself to break out of this narrowly proscribed life. My outburst needed to happen. I had a sense that *something* was changing and that I was too.

In 1962, just a month after I left Oregon and arrived in San Francisco, and before any drug experimentation, I received my first paycheck at the law firm where I worked. I wanted to celebrate and go out for lunch. Bruce, the only attorney there friendly with us secretaries, suggested that Barbara and I go to Jack's. We found it in a little alley. It didn't look like much either outside or inside. Jack's had probably been around since the Gold Rush and so had the waiters. They wore tight white jackets and carried a crisp white napkin draped over one arm, something I had seen only in movies.

We were the only women there. The other diners looked important. I sensed their power in their dark suits and conservative ties. Conversations were hushed. I was uncomfortable and felt out of place. Bruce was a nice guy. I didn't think he would set us up, but I wasn't sure why he had recommended Jack's.

I was uncertain whether we would even be served, but we were. As we were eating, a group of six arrived and was seated at a reserved table behind us. Then I heard a man start to sing. When I turned around he was handing the one woman at the table a long-stemmed red rose as he sang "Thank Heaven for Little Girls." It was Maurice Chevalier. I was in awe, not only because he was famous but because the woman was so elegantly dressed at lunch in her black dress and coifed blonde hair. We all applauded and resumed eating. I'll never forget what I had for lunch—lamb stew. I knew better than to ask for an autograph. Later I found out through Herb Caen's daily column in the San Francisco *Chronicle* that Maurice Chevalier and Louis Lurie, the owner of the Mark Hopkins Hotel, were good friends and lunched often at Jack's. Lurie was probably among those at the table. My attorney friend Bruce had steered us well. We had hit the jackpot as far as I was concerned, a mere legal secretary rubbing elbows with a famous person without even trying. So this is what it would be like living in San Francisco.

I was learning to be a San Francisco sophisticate. I bought beautiful clothes, lightened my hair and attended swank Young Republican cocktail parties held in hotel ballrooms or atmospheric former fire stations. At one of the parties I met John, a law student whom I dated for a while. One evening at his house he got too drunk to drive me home and I had to stay over. He was living with his parents in St. Francis Wood, one of San Francisco's most elegant neighborhoods. Governor Edmund Brown lived across the street. John's parents were away. We were having late Sunday morning coffee in the living room when Kathleen Brown and some other members of the Governor's family dropped in unexpectedly. It was all very casual; they were simply neighbors. John was comfortable having the Browns there, but I was not. I had no change of clothes, and John had given me a robe to wear. I remember it was thin and slippery and didn't conceal me very well. I looked terrible and was so embarrassed that after introductions I tried to disappear into the sofa.

Another time I rubbed elbows with Margot St. James. A friend invited me out on a Tuesday evening to meet her. I had heard of Margot, organizer of The Hookers' Ball and founder of COYOTE (Call Off Your Old Tired Ethics), an organization advocating legalization of prostitution. She and Herb Caen were friends; he often mentioned her in his column.

We parked on Folsom Street, a decrepit part of town, in front of a tall white Victorian. This was before south of Market became SOMA, which now means So Only the Most Affluent. We climbed creaky wooden stairs to the fifth floor and joined about twenty other people waiting to meet Margot. When the host appeared he rolled back the floor to expose a huge hot tub, large enough for all of us. We stripped to our birthday suits and eased into the hot water. I wondered how this old wooden building could support the weight of all that water. I had not noticed the trapeze hanging over the hot tub, but when Margot arrived she expertly caught the bar and swung back and forth above the tub and bathers, bare bottom hanging in full view. I was amazed that anyone could be so at ease naked with strangers. She obviously was enjoying herself, pleased to be the guest of honor, pleased to have an appreciative audience. I guess to say I "rubbed elbows" with her is not quite accurate.

Undressed and through no plan of my own, I seemed to be meeting persons of note. I suspected I would continue to meet more interesting people as a twenty-something in San Francisco, but I preferred that next time I would be fully clothed.

Time came for my first two-week vacation in 1963 after working for a year in San Francisco, and friend Sheila proposed a trip to Mexico. We would go to Mexico City, Taxco, Cuernavaca, Acapulco and Puerto Vallarta. Sheila and Jean worked at the Almaden Wines sales office in San Francisco. We were all part of the self-proclaimed Green Street Gang, a group of friends who lived in apartments along Green Street in Pacific Heights. The owner of Almaden, Louis Benoist, owned a hotel in Puerto Vallarta where we could get a break on the rate. We would end our trip there. Sheila was fluent in Spanish, having worked for the U.S. Government in Spain for several years.

Sheila, Jean and I arrived in Mexico City where we had reservations at the Geneva Hotel, which we dubbed "menopause manor." Most of the guests were middle aged; we were in our twenties. The lobby, a light-filled atrium, was sedate and leafy. We were looking for more excitement, so we taxied to the much grander Sheraton where we happened to meet three young Mexican men in the bar who were also looking for action. In barely ten minutes they had joined us and we had paired up.

I like to believe we were prizes, the men were so attentive. Three young, pretty blonde *Americanas*. They hardly let us out of their sight, and we went out every evening.

Oscar Legaspe was "mine," an *abogado* (attorney), my third word in Spanish, after *muchas gracias*. I don't

79

remember what Jorge or Felipe did, but their jobs didn't seem to demand much of them. We were out very late every night. We were escorted to some of the best places in and around Mexico City. I especially remember the Jacaranda, where we danced for hours. They took us for an afternoon of bullfighting and lunch. There were a few strips of something I didn't recognize in my salad. Silky white with a tiny black dot at one end. I pushed the baby eels aside. We drove outside the city to climb the Pyramid of the Sun. My lack of Spanish and Oscar's lack of English didn't matter much. Somehow, we understood each other, or thought we did. Oscar was courtly and gentlemanly. It was like being in a Jane Austin novel, our relationship restrained and quietly exciting. I was treated like a princess, with respect and admiration, as though I were someone very special. I saw Oscar as someone special too, a sensitive, worldly man.

When Oscar took me to Mexico City's huge Chapultepec Park, he showed me a stone house where he had spent summers as a child. He said the house had once been part of his family's estate. Some years back the government had decided to redistribute holdings of large landowners. His family's land in the park had been confiscated. Oscar looked wistful and sad as he told me this. It was a cloudy day, and I have a lovely picture of him, one leg propped on a low stone wall, looking as misty and brooding as the weather.

During the day when the men were at their jobs we went sightseeing, shopping and exploring in the hotel district. One morning I went to a nearby restaurant alone for breakfast. Ordered shrimp *en brochette* and coffee. I was one of few diners and the three mariachis serenaded me at my table. For breakfast! The dollar was strong, and we could splurge. I thought this was the way Mexicans lived— color, art and music everywhere, lush flowers, exquisite food. Then I saw a ragged woman sitting on the pavement with her hand out, a naked, newborn baby lying beside her. The baby had diarrhea. I knew the baby was dying. I passed by. I will never forget the pleading in her eyes.

We went by ourselves to Acapulco but planned to reconnect with Oscar, Jorge and Felipe in Puerto Vallarta at the end of our trip. We arrived in Puerto Vallarta and checked into the Oceana Hotel. The open-air *cabanas* were up a steep hill, bedrooms on one level, the bathroom and shower on the next. In the outdoor shower, I could peek through a curtain of bougainvillea and see Banderas Bay. I vowed one day I would have an outdoor shower of my own. There's nothing quite so lovely. It's still on my bucket list.

Three days lying on the beach swimming, sunning and exploring, besotted with love and margaritas. Tearful goodbyes. Yes, I'll write.

When I returned to work I was asked about my vacation. I burst into tears.

I took beginning Spanish that summer. Oscar wrote to me in clumsy English. I responded in awkward Spanish. How romantic can you be when all you have are words from a beginning Spanish text?

We three returned to Mexico the following year. And it was as though we had not had a year's separation. One evening Oscar drove me in his blue Volkswagen to a bluff overlooking the lights of Mexico City. A popular viewpoint, it was also a makeout spot. It took us a while before we could locate a parking space. I think we were kissing when there was a knock on the window. A cop. I could feel the tension in the conversation but couldn't understand what they were saying. Oscar leaned over and pulled out cash from the glove box to give to the cop. After the cop left he told me he had given him about twenty dollars. I asked Oscar about the small handgun I had seen in the glove box. He said it was necessary protection and added that Mexico was so corrupt that anyone with any resources put his money in a Swiss bank.

The next to last evening in Mexico City Oscar took me to San Angel Inn overlooking the city for dinner. A traditional seventeenth century hacienda had been converted into an elegant restaurant, with exposed dark ceiling beams and crystal chandeliers. The waiters wore tight jackets with two rows of silver buttons. Mariachis in equally elaborate costumes serenaded. Impeccable service. I was being romanced, and it was working. I was floating. The restaurant is still there, rated number eight among Mexico City's twelve hundred-plus restaurants.

The last night our Mexican boyfriends took us to a house the three of them owned. They retained a live-in couple to maintain it. As unmarried, well-born Mexican men, they would live with their parents until marriage. They took their dates to this house for privacy. Oscar did try to put the make on me, but we both quickly pulled away. I think he thought it was expected of him, as a macho Mexican man. That out of the way, we could resume conducting our chaste romance, confined to exchanging longing glances, kisses and warm hugs.

That summer the letter-writing slowed and we eventually lost touch. I have looked for him on social media but have not found him.

## The Oracle of Delphi

I was still trussed up and working at the management consulting firm when my roommate and friend from college, Molly, suggested I might want to go with her sister Kay on a trip through Europe, one of those twenty-five-countries-in-twenty-eight-days trips. I was about the same age as the length of the trip. It was no problem to go at that pace. The first hurdle was to get the month off from work. They said yes. Kay and I met her Manhattan friend, Muffie, in Paris and we started touring using *Europe on $5 a Day*.

We designed our itinerary as we went along, roaming through France, Germany and Italy. After Italy, we decided to go on to Greece. We landed in Athens at dusk. It was August. Stifling. No reservations. In the dark, we stumbled up the stairs to a cheap hotel with a double bed for the three of us, dumped our bags, and went out to find dinner. Exhausted by the heat, we climbed to a rooftop *taverna*, and there, almost close enough to touch, was the Parthenon, lit with golden floodlights in all its democratic glory. A trio was playing Greek music on bouzoukis, something like a mandolin but pitched lower and with a metallic sound. A beautiful blonde woman in black danced the handkerchief dance. We were transfixed. We didn't care if the three of us had to sleep with no air conditioning crosswise on a small bed.

Before leaving Athens to sail through the islands, we decided to visit the Oracle of Delphi, several hours by car from Athens. At the car rental, we met

Jan from Amsterdam, a man also in his twenties, who was planning the same day trip, so we joined up and shared the cost. A long drive through rough, rocky terrain marked by scores of tiny white-domed chapels, large enough for the private devotions of only one or two people. In Delphi, we spent the day exploring the amphitheater and the stone chambers where the Oracle went into trance to answer pressing questions of state. We breathed deeply to capture any remaining trance-inducing vapors. We cooled off in the stream where she is said to have bathed. We spent the day picnicking and drinking retsina, hoping the Oracle would appear to answer our own pressing questions. Today, this area is closed to the public, except for the crumbling amphitheater. There's no chance of encountering the Oracle or bathing in her stream. The public has been barred.

It was dark when we started back to Athens, drunk not with vapors but sun, heat and retsina wine. About ten o'clock we saw a banner strung across the road advertising a roadside restaurant. A farmer and his wife had set up a picnic table in their field. Tablecloth, lanterns. They served spit-roasted lamb with fresh rosemary, potatoes and vegetables, all from their farm. A hearty, heavenly meal.

Jan had flirted with me during the day, and now we snuggled in the back seat of the Volkswagen bug. He was a sculptor and teacher who had been traveling the Holy Land, Turkey, and Greece before returning home to be married. He didn't seem very eager to get home or to marry. As we neared the city he whispered, "You come with me." I couldn't think of a reason not to, so we dropped Kay and Muffie off at the hotel. Jan drove confidently up the hill which dominates the city. It was almost dawn. We made love in the shrubbery on the hillside of the Acropolis just below that same golden Parthenon. As the sun rose I could see that the bushes were full of people doing the same thing. The exotic romance of the setting overwhelmed any sense of impropriety I might have had. Perhaps I had sniffed the Oracle's vapors after all.

Jan gave me a memento—a simple silver cross studded with a piece of turquoise he had purchased in Damascus. I kept it for many years.

## CUTTING LOOSE

Gil, my boyfriend at the time, invited me to a concert in a small, gray concrete basement amphitheater in Sproul Hall on the Berkeley campus. It was 1963. I was insulted he would take me to hear anyone so raspy and tuneless. It was Bob Dylan singing "The Times They Are a-Changin'."

Things were changing, thank God.

A band with a strange name, Jefferson Airplane, played at The Matrix at Union and Fillmore, a block from my apartment. One Sunday I saw an ad in the *Chronicle*'s Pink Section for The Trips Festival at Longshoreman's Hall. Ken Kesey and the Merry Pranksters, among others, organized the event. Kesey had been a senior at the University of Oregon when I was a sophomore. He was an odd duck. I wanted to go to the Trips Festival but not alone. My roommates did not seem to recognize this was something significant. Later I heard the Kool-Aid was spiked with acid. You probably know the story.

And then I met Mike who first turned me on to marijuana. He was an electrical engineer in the process of dropping out. He had grown a beard and was living in a dingy apartment in North Beach. He was moving onto an old boat he was restoring docked at Gate 5 in Sausalito. For his moving-out party he had taped paper to the walls. Everyone was stoned and we drew all over the walls. This was fun, exciting, liberating. It was stepping out of line, like being late with the coffee but without consequences. I was beginning to change my opinion that the only attractive people were those who lived in Pacific Heights, dressed well, worked on Montgomery Street, played bridge, and went to Young Republican parties at the St. Francis. After not breathing for so long I felt liberated—from tight dresses, girdles, having to call men "mister" and fearing to speak my mind.

Driving stoned with Mike across the Golden Gate Bridge to his boat at Gate 5 was magic, lights so bright they cut my eyes. Mike later suggested I try LSD. I had read about Aldous Huxley's experience with mescaline in *The Doors of Perception*. One day Mike told me he had some acid and had arranged with friends to be our guides at their home in Fairfax. I was ready. They were familiar with the experience and would take care of us.

It was a quiet sunny Sunday. I was glad for the fence around the small cottage and garden. I knew it would keep us from wandering off. Mike and I sat together on the front steps. I swallowed a small, white tablet and waited. I had no idea what to expect.

Then I noticed thousands of sparkling, jeweled insects flying around me—emeralds, rubies, diamonds, sapphires, topaz. The air was so thick with them that I didn't want to breathe in a mouthful accidentally, so I held my hand over my mouth. They were both bugs and gems at the same time. I thought about how crunchy in my mouth they would be. I was aware I was hallucinating but I did wonder if they were always there and I just hadn't noticed them. All this beauty in the air, the world full of precious gems just there for the taking.

Our guides led us to the bathroom to look in the mirror. I was afraid to look at myself but I did look at Mike. Instead of his Irish handsomeness I saw him as an ape. It was frightening. His lips were tight over his teeth, much sharper and larger than normal, sneering. I thought he might be dangerous. I knew I needed to stop looking at him or I could lose control and give in to fear. I can see now how people on acid can find themselves in terrifying places. Fortunately, I kept my balance. Throughout the entire trip I remained more or less intact, my watching, commenting self always there.

We were given fruit. I was sitting on the ground and opened the orange, deep into the trip. I began to mash the orange, mixing the juice into the dirt, making it nice and brown and squishy. I was playing with my feces. I was a toddler and enjoying it immensely. I noticed it did not smell.

I began to cry sometime that afternoon and cried for what seemed like hours. I didn't want to stop. I cried because I felt that everything actually was all right and that everything was always going to be okay for me. It was wonderful to feel confident down to my marrow that everything would be okay in a great big whole-world way. Never had I felt such rock-bottom assurance. I cried big tears of relief.

It was now early evening, still light out, and some neighbors stopped by. I was still hallucinating and I saw the face of one of the men, possibly another dangerous animal. His skull appeared terribly distorted, his forehead thick with bony mounds. This time I didn't wait to find out if he was dangerous or not. I crawled under a concrete garden bench for safety and crouched there until they left. I was grateful they were respectful and left me alone. They knew we were tripping.

Mike took me home and stayed with me so I wouldn't be alone when the LSD wore off. I suspect it was quite a powerful dose. The next morning I didn't feel different; I was disappointed. Talking about it later with friends I was aware of how smug I felt. I enjoyed shocking them. It took a long time, though, to work through how much the experience had changed me.

I had been cracked open and could no longer pretend. I knew I had been living a lie that I knew who I was. I did not. I was a frightened, empty person who made myself up as I went along. If I were going to a party I took a little square pink diet pill (amphetamine) just to build my courage. To try to be someone. I was frightened because there was so little of me. I learned to stop judging others by what they wore, what they drove and where they lived. To look past all that into the person in front of me. I learned to think through my opinions more carefully. I learned I am valuable, that God-or-Whatever loves me, that I was hiding a mountain of hurt that had to be healed.

But before that I had more sixties adventures.

REPRODUCTION

I think it started in early high school. Debilitating cramps so bad the vice principal Mr. Lind would have to drive me home. I was humiliated but too sick to object. Everyone would KNOW. Mother would meet me at the gate and help me up the stairs and down the hall to the bathroom where my body emptied itself out at both ends. I think I fainted once, falling off the toilet.

Then to bed with the heating pad and Midol, both ineffective. Today I imagine it might be like going into labor—every month.

When I got my first period and told my mother, she announced it in the kitchen that evening to the family. She said, "Carol became a young woman today." I was mortified. Sex did not exist in my family. And this was about SEX. The icy tone in her voice has always troubled me. It implied, "And what are you going to do about that now?" I could not let myself think about what she might have meant. Was she directing it at me, at my father, at herself?

I got pregnant the first time I had sex. This was pre-pill. I told boyfriend Gil, the one who had taken me to hear Bob Dylan. He waffled. I didn't know how he felt about me, and he wouldn't say. Marriage was not mentioned. I went to several gynecologists in San Francisco for confirmation and asked, timidly, if there was anything they might do to "help me." It was understood what "help" meant. Each in turn solemnly shook his head.

Gil was elusive in other ways besides how he felt about me. He claimed to be working on an important project, one he kept in a locked closet in the hallway of his one-room apartment. The implication was that it would make his fortune. As often as I asked and promised to keep the secret, he would never tell me what was in that locked closet. I suspect it was as nonexistent as his affection for me.

He did offer to help me. I could live out the duration of my pregnancy in his parents' Southern California motel. I visualized myself hiding out, peeking from behind the draperies, never going out. I declined his offer. At three months pregnant the help I did accept was a trip to Tijuana. I was grateful he knew where to go. He had taken someone down that back alley before.

I was certain the flight attendants knew exactly where we were going and for what. I brought $300 in cash with me, the price Gil had negotiated. I think it was evening when we arrived in Tijuana. We had to be very careful not to arouse any suspicion about our destination. We were simply tourists.

The makeshift operating room was the doctor's crowded little living room. Thankfully, I was out completely during the procedure and I remember very little afterwards, except that Gil had to struggle to get the drugged me into a taxi, to the airport, onto the plane. This time I was too dopey to care what the flight attendants thought.

Gil took me to stay with him in Mill Valley that night and then home to San Francisco the next morning.

After a visit to a San Francisco gynecologist to treat the infection, I was fine. Except I wasn't. I was in a daze during the entire ordeal, from discovery to recovery. I was stunned by Gil's casual dismissal. I wanted him to marry me to save me from shame, not because I was in love with him. Before *Roe v. Wade*, a woman pregnant and unmarried could be doomed for life. My father might never have spoken to me again. At the very least our relationship would have been badly damaged.

Gil said he would pay me back for the cost of the abortion. I would check the mailbox every day after work. Intermittently there would be an envelope with money in it that he delivered himself. It took him a year to pay me back. I don't remember dating anyone that year.

I had no contact with Gil until about ten years later when he contacted me and asked me to meet him. I didn't know what he wanted. He told me he had married a flight attendant. He was as uncommunicative as he had been when I knew him. I cut the meeting short. He was a stranger.

I was surprised to learn that my roommate had been to Tijuana earlier, having heard of a doctor there through a coworker. Apparently, it was relatively easy to find one. And when *Ms. Magazine* asked for names of women who had had abortions, I sent mine in. In the tiniest print possible so that all submissions could be included, thousands of women gave their names.

I was right on time with menopause—in my early fifties. I was determined never to have a hot flash, since I had been hot all my life, my face dripping with perspiration. I was taking hormone replacements to prevent the unpleasant episodes I saw others suffering. One night I awoke with violent cramps. I staggered to the bathroom where I had nausea and diarrhea and came close to fainting. I was thirteen once again. The same thing happened two weeks later. And that was my menopause. It went out as forcefully as it came in. And I've never had a hot flash.

## Working at Drake-Holter Publishing

I ended my eventful but ultimately suffocating five years on Montgomery Street and found a job in North Beach. It was my version of dropping out, which meant wearing relaxed, casual clothes; addressing bosses by their first name; seeking out creative people; and using mind-altering substances.

Drake-Holter Publishing was particularly attractive to me because it was located in the Columbus Tower building, the white, triangular Victorian building at the corner of Columbus and Kearney, full of atmosphere and history and not far from Melvin Belli's office. At that time, the building was owned by the Kingston Trio. The Trio had a recording studio in the basement but I never saw them. The building had a colorful history, housing not only musicians but notorious politicians of an earlier era. One such person, Abe Ruef, had commissioned the building in 1905, but he was delayed from occupying it, first, because of earthquake damage and, second, until he had served a sentence for bribery in San Quentin. The offices were awkwardly configured within the triangular building, and I wondered why there were as many as four doors in one of our small top-floor offices. It occurred to me we could be housed in a former brothel, the many doors allowing for escape in case of a raid, or in case Abe Ruef needed to make a hasty escape. The building is now owned by Francis Ford Coppola and houses his film production company, American Zoetrope.

Herb Drake had retired from J. Walter Thompson advertising in New York. In 1968, he was following his dream of owning a publishing business. His magazine, called, simply, *Living in California*, described everything the large numbers of people moving to California in the sixties needed to know about life in California—housing, schools, jobs, recreation, politics. Dick Holter sold advertising. Not a moneymaker, the magazine lasted only a year.

We had a wonderful time during that short year. Herb would generously host his staff at lunch at Cecilia Chiang's legendary Mandarin, Chinatown's best restaurant, for extravagant northern Chinese food and martini lunches. He financed photo shoots to places all over Northern California. I would go as assistant to Ted, the editor. Ted was also my boyfriend. Herb authorized buying photos from the best professional photographers, whom Ted knew from his newspaper days.

We all sensed we were on a sinking ship. For one thing, none of us seemed to have much to do. Both principals were usually out of the office. The rest of us would try to stay busy but there wasn't even make-work to do. I tried not to think what I would do when the magazine folded, so I focused instead on enjoying extended lunches in North Beach and going out to the bars after work with Ted, who knew where the most interesting regulars drank. Most of them were artists, journalists, or photographers he had known as editor for five years of *Bonanza*, the *San Francisco Chronicle*'s Sunday magazine section.

I was acutely uncomfortable being seen with Ted, who was sixteen years older than I and looked it. He kept a close watch on me at work. I dared not flirt with the young, attractive paste-up artist. In fact, I hardly talked with him, fearing Ted's reaction.

Ted was slovenly; his clothes looked like they came from the sale bin at Goodwill. He didn't seem to care. He was divorced and supported four children, not very successfully. He drank too much and smoked. A poor money manager, he traded his paintings for necessities—doctors' visits, a set of dentures, his bar bill. He had been a talented photographer, fine arts painter, jazz trumpeter, an award-winning filmmaker. Several of his paintings are in the collection of a Midwest museum. All that was in the past by the time I knew him. Ted was on a downslide in his life and I could sense the same in myself. Once we stayed in the office overnight drinking bourbon out of the bottle and sleeping it off all night on the floor. This was my nadir. As the magazine was sinking, so was I.

I usually spent weekends with Ted at his apartment in Novato, but one summer Sunday I was preparing to leave early for an afternoon barbecue in the Santa Cruz Mountains. I had been wanting to end the relationship for some time, and this was my opportunity. I was afraid of Ted, and I knew I was acting boldly while on his turf. Only now I realize he was controlling and subtly menacing, but I could not allow myself to recognize it when I was dating him. As I was showering and preparing to leave, Ted forced open the locked bathroom door and yanked back the shower curtain, scaring me nearly to death. I couldn't believe he would do this. I was frightened but resolved. I wondered if he would prevent me from leaving, but he did not. I dressed quickly and left.

I had escaped, for the time being.

My hosts were hippies living in the Santa Cruz Mountains. They had raised a lamb and wanted to experience food at its most fundamental level—from birth to slaughtering to butchering to roasting. No Safeway Styrofoam packages here. By Sunday afternoon when I arrived, the lamb had been slaughtered and skinned. Thank God I had missed the drama of the kill.

On the way out to the back of the house where the lamb was roasting on a spit over a wood fire on the bare earth, I tried not to look at the bloody fleece in the laundry tubs. I feigned nonchalance, hoping I wouldn't be sick. I imagined I saw the skins moving. At the same time, as an experienced knitter I wondered what would become of all that wool.

I made it out to the spit without being sick and took my turn at the crank. I quelled my squeamishness because I wanted to savor this ritual as it has been practiced for thousands of years. As we waited for the lamb to roast, we practiced another ritual of sipping peyote tea. The hours slipped smoothly by, and the lamb was done. It was then evening, a clear starry night. We stood around the roasted sacrifice as we feasted on chunks of delicious meat we pulled off with our fingers. I can't remember a finer meal.

I saw Ted a few more times. One afternoon he was at my apartment at Pacific and Fillmore in San Francisco, and I told him I wanted to end the relationship. Before I knew what was happening, he had me pinned on my back on my bed with his hands around my throat. I looked straight into his eyes and said, "Ted, what are you doing?" He hesitated a moment, then let go. That was the last time I saw him.

Ted had given me several paintings. One, in black and white, he had painted from a snapshot of me, wincing, skinny-dipping in a very cold Eel River. Another, painted before I met him, I gave to his son Mark in 2010, whom I found through the Internet living in Clear Lake. I was surprised he remembered me. He was grateful to have one of his father's paintings, having lost his others in a flood. I kept an earlier piece and paid $1,200 to have it restored. It's faintly reminiscent of a Chagall.

## NUDITY

Nudity was big in the sixties, and I did my share of taking my clothes off. Nudity was another way to erase class and power differences, so when I found a massage class with its politics in order—students and teachers all naked—I signed up. I don't know where I got the idea I could be comfortable sitting in the nude on the instructor's living room floor with a dozen other similarly unclothed strangers. I gazed with as soft a focus as I could to avoid looking at anyone. It was a leap I was having difficulty making—oiling, rubbing and kneading a stranger while I was naked. I discovered I didn't care enough about class and power differences to become a naked masseuse. One session was enough and I left the class.

A woman friend invited me to another nude event. A NUDE, SINGLES PARTY. A home on Park Boulevard. A Wednesday evening I believe. Fifteen dollars at the door. This was a completely cuckoo idea, but I didn't want to appear prudish so I told my friend I would go with her to lend support.

Down the walk and onto the porch. I lagged behind and tried to duck away in the dark but then remembered my friend had the car. Oh my God! The living room was full of naked bodies, mostly men, sprawled over every surface, displaying themselves. I felt I was on the primate island at the zoo. Right then and there I made fast friends with my inner prude and quickly made my way through the hairy, naked bodies up a few stairs to an outside deck. There were so many people on the small deck I had trouble squeezing in. I wasn't the only single there who wanted to start out a bit more slowly getting to know someone, maybe over coffee with clothes on.

The best time I had with my clothes mostly off was at an event in the Haight. Pierre, a stained glass artist friend from Montreal, had heard about a party and suggested he paint my body for the occasion. Oooh, yes. I stood on a high stool for hours while he did his stained-glass designs. He worked so long I thought the party would be over by the time we got there. My entire body was a piece of geometrical art drawn with red, green, blue and black markers. I wore a backless halter top and a wraparound skirt which I could easily flip open to reveal the designs on my legs.

We climbed to the top floor of a Victorian where people were dancing in a big open attic. Band playing, people mellow, soft lighting. I began to dance and the floor cleared. Alone and free, I took off my top and danced that wonderful art.

As we were leaving, someone called out, "Your woman sure can dance." He said nothing about the art. I loved it. I had never felt so supple, so easy in my body.

More recently, on vacation in Puerto Vallarta with a woman friend, I suggested we pose as Manet's *Olympia* and take snapshots before we went out for the evening. You know, the painting of a dark-haired nude reclining on an embroidered shawl with a large red flower tucked behind her ear looking directly out at the viewer. Puerto Vallarta is a party town, a place where you can really strut your stuff. We had brought with us all the silver and turquoise jewelry we owned

101

and bought more from the vendors on the beach. One vendor in particular had especially well-designed pieces. We were good customers. I had perhaps fourteen bracelets and as many necklaces.

So, minus clothes but laden with all our jewelry, we took turns posing on the garish green and yellow bedspread in our budget hotel room and took photos of each other. Maybe it was the missing shawl or the missing flower, but we looked plain and disappointingly plump. All that jewelry could not compete with Manet's slender, sensuous model wearing a simple black ribbon around her neck and a flower in her hair.

## Druid Heights
### Part One—The Memory

In the early 1970s, a friend invited me to spend a Sunday afternoon in Marin County. The invitation was vague: something about a hot tub, a new thing. We drove to Muir Woods, then turned right up a narrow gravel road just short of the entrance to the national monument. At the end of the rutted road was a clearing with a few houses and barns. Unless they knew where to go, the thousands of visitors to Muir Woods would never have guessed this settlement was there. It was known as Druid Heights. The name evoked mystery and excitement.

Our host that day had access to one of the homes in Druid Heights, a circular structure with a mushroom-like overhanging roof. The rooms seemed to drift one into the other, as dreamily as fog in the redwoods. I especially remember the kitchen cabinets. The half doors were a graceful sculpture of lacy wooden branch-like forms. The bathtub was a deep oval of sculpted cement studded with pieces of broken pottery and glass jewels. The dining table was almost even with the plush carpeted floor over a deep well so one could sit comfortably at the table. There was a meditation room with an altar and a large round window.

The hot tub sat on the hillside among the tall redwoods and aromatic eucalyptus near this fantastical house overlooking the hills which descended in railroad-tie steps to the ocean. We could hear waves but not see them in the fog. We took off our clothes and slipped in. How delicious, to be naked with strangers in the woods on a Sunday afternoon at a place called Druid Heights.

This magical place was unbelievably strange and exotic in the seventies. We were told that an artist living in Hawaii owned the house. When he died, it would become the property of the U.S. Forest Service because of its proximity to Muir Woods. Its current tenant, who was not at home that Sunday, was Alan Watts, who had named it Mandala House.

Alan Watts was responsible for introducing large numbers of people to Eastern mysticism in the sixties. I never missed his Sunday evening program on KPFA if I could help it. An admired spiritual teacher, Alan Watts was also an ardent hedonist, loving women, wine and parties. He died in 1973, probably from an excess of alcohol. Some of his ashes are scattered at Druid Heights.

Before writing about my visit that long-ago Sunday, I wanted to find out more about Druid Heights. I struck gold on the Internet when I found a book, *The Visionary State: a Journey Through California's Spiritual Landscape*, by Erik Davis. Mandala House is there with pictures and a history of Druid Heights. A woman had purchased the property in the 1950s and named it. Word got around, and it became a draw for artists, writers, sex rebels and seekers. A few of the residents or visitors were Gary Snyder, Dizzy Gillespie, Neil Young and Tom Robbins.

On the Web I found the craftsman, Ed Stiles, who had built Mandala House, and I emailed and asked him how I might find it to refresh my memory.

He still lived in Druid Heights and invited me to visit. I was thrilled.

Part Two—The Revisit

In May 2012, I returned from a visit to Druid Heights, with a renewed appreciation for the phenomenon of memory, not for its accuracy but for its creativity.

Druid Heights was easy to find with Ed Stiles' directions. I invited artist friend Jane to go with me. We turned left, not right, as the road is marked on my AAA map. The mile-long entry road is almost giving way in places. A warning sign says "Keep Far to the Left." We crept along, hugging the uphill side of the road.

After the tense mile, it was hard to evoke the sense of mystery I had remembered. In the bright spring sunlight, it was just a place in the woods. The Druids were gone. Ed Stiles, the Mandala House builder, came out to greet us and invited us in for tea. He had built his own house overlooking a canyon. It was dark and had that sense of growing organically as the need arose during the forty-seven years he has lived in Druid Heights:  a bedroom added for his children as they came, and a laundry room now adjacent to the kitchen when his wife was no longer comfortable descending a ship's ladder through a trapdoor in the kitchen floor to the washer in a space under the kitchen.

He then led us down the hill through the eucalyptus. Mandala House was hardly what I remembered. It was small and cramped, no flow to the rooms because there was only one main room. The current resident seemed not at all Zen-like, with her stuff piled haphazardly everywhere. There was no meditation room with the round window. It was in the Moon Temple, another structure at Druid Heights which we did not visit. The biggest disappointment of all were the kitchen cabinets—plain flat wood doors. The only sculpture in the kitchen was a dramatic wood frame encircling a large skylight in a flame-like design. The bathtub was of cement and oval, but there were no encrusted shards of pottery or glass jewels. Just gray cement. The woman who lives there said the kitchen and bathroom were as they always had been. She has lived at Druid Heights for at least thirty years.

I refuse to let go of my memory of Druid Heights, much preferring my memory's artful amendments to Mandala House. I had transported the carving from around the skylight, made it lighter and more graceful and put it on the kitchen cabinets. Imagination is not concerned with practicalities such as how to remove plates and cups from behind sharply-pointed carved wood tendrils. I had made the Moon Temple and Mandala House into one, melding the meditation room with its altar and round window with flowing rooms of pristine Zen-ness, graceful carvings and a jeweled bathtub. It was a rare opportunity to observe the unreliability and creativity of memory at work. I am tempted to avoid other challenges to my memories. Many are full of rich detail, and I fear that in the bright light of the present, they might be exposed as dull and plain. I need that richness, even if it was induced by whatever was infused in the tea served to us in that long ago visit.

## ON THE BUS TO MEXICO

I was working at a temporary job when coworker Norma told me she would be leaving to take a month-long bus trip through Mexico in mid-December. She had seen a notice on the Co-op bulletin board advertising for passengers. The Co-op bulletin board on Telegraph Avenue in Berkeley was the Internet of the day—the place to go for whatever you needed. I was 38 and more than ready for my next adventure. I called Bob and arranged to meet him at his bus, a beat-up, thirty-year-old school bus painted a chalky baby blue. Bob looked pretty beat up, too, with his wild hair and beard and rumpled clothes. The bus looked as though the sides would fall off at the first bump. It was dirty inside. He assured me it was safe and, yes, he would clean it before the trip. Bill Two said he would like to go, so we quit our jobs, paid our $300 each and packed up. I was doing admin assist work for an Asian woman who was using grant money to do I-don't-know-what and who was distressed when I gave my notice that I had not organized her several voluminous address books stuffed with business cards and phone numbers on scrap paper. Bill Two was working unhappily at Lawrence Livermore Labs. He told me he fell asleep most afternoons.

Bob the bus driver had once been an IBM professional, as had Bill Two. He had dropped out as a number of professionals did at that time. His speech was garbled. None of us could understand what he was saying. I think he wanted it that way so he could have complete control of the trip.

We embarked from Berkeley. Bob had not cleaned the bus. I really didn't want to sleep on the floor, but others had claimed the benches at the back of the bus before we got there. The only remaining available space to roll out our sleeping bags was down the middle aisle. I'm sure that's how I picked up scabies.

We were a typically varied Bay Area bunch. There was Norma the social worker; Pam the librarian, with her young son; Bill Two, the recovering IBM computer scientist who had nothing in common with Bob, the driver; and me, the admin. assist. There were also three San Francisco call girls who were members of COYOTE. Two of the COYOTEs were originally from Mexico City and were going to see their wealthy boyfriends to earn some much-needed cash. The boyfriends were in jail but were allowed conjugal visits.

The trip was getting interesting.

Bob started out driving and then Bill took over for a four-hour shift. That was the only time Bob let Bill or anyone else drive—from Berkeley to Acapulco and back—fueled as he was with amphetamines and tequila. Bob was a very good driver in spite of his intoxication. I was surprised I could be a relaxed passenger. Most of the time.

Bob wanted to meet the "real" people of Mexico. That meant heading to the least picturesque, poorest, dirtiest parts of Mexico. We spent Christmas eve aboard the bus parked in a vacant parking lot in

Puebla in the mountains not far from Mexico City, eating a cold supper. One day we had just cleared one of the numerous *Federale* (federal police) checkpoints and found a place to park for the night when the *Federales* returned and invited Bob to party with them later that evening. He was overjoyed. He would finally be able to party with "the people." I remember waking up as he was trying to get back into the bus at 3 a.m. We always locked it from the inside at night.

As we were getting ready to leave in the morning the *Federales* were back, this time not to party but to search our bus for drugs. They were armed. Who knows what Bob had told them in his drunken night of conviviality? They took a long time going through the bus searching our various backpacks, boxes and duffel bags, slowly, methodically. We sat still and straight as innocents. I hoped the women from Mexico City were diplomatic and deferential as they spoke in Spanish to the *Federales*. They finally gave up in disgust and let us go.

Thank God someone had hidden their marijuana very well. I shudder to think what would have happened if the *Federales* had found it. I've wondered how long I might have spent in some remote Mexican prison. I didn't know who had it and did not want to know.

The trip was getting scary.

One day we were driving through the mountains of Michoacan in that dilapidated school bus over a winding mountain road with no shoulder and no guardrail, looking down into a deep canyon. I was so tense I could barely breathe. I told myself to just relax and enjoy the scenery, since there was nothing I could do. It worked.

We headed to Zijuataneo, at that time nothing but a small, coastal fishing village. Bob had heard about an American couple living in the jungle a few miles outside Zijuataneo, and we lurched through the jungle over a barely passable road to find them. They were anticipating an influx of tourists to the area and were building an open air bar and dance floor but had run out of money. (They were ten years too early.) She left her boyfriend and joined our bus, broke and with no contacts in the Bay Area. I was impressed at how the COYOTEs took her in, eager to help her get established as a high-class call girl when they got back. I won't go into detail about some of the tricks of the trade I overheard. I was surprised by how encouraging and helpful the COYOTEs were to the newcomer. They really wanted her in the sisterhood. I also got the impression that if a woman were attractive it was a *very* lucrative calling.

Halfway through the trip Bill and I decided to leave the bus and travel on our own for the remaining two weeks. We had brought extra cash in case we wanted to bail. I had seen enough of the poverty of Mexico. We stayed in resorts, spas and boutique hotels. I finally got rid of the scabies. I barely remember the upscale hotels we stayed in, but I have vivid memories of those first two weeks on the bus. I learned a lot about letting go. I learned I could go for days without a shower and be reasonably comfortable. I learned I could eat a meal without a napkin. I learned I could chat with a prostitute as with any other person. I learned I had a taste for risk and adventure. I learned I could entrust my life to a guy driving an old bus through the mountains and survive.

As for the second half of the trip, I heard later from Norma the social worker that the only time there was any problem was a flat tire in San Jose, the last fifty miles from Berkeley.

In the 1970s, when I was moving around a lot, I decided to try communal living. Many people were forming group houses, and when I saw an ad for one on the Co-op bulletin board I joined one. The advertised house was a barge permanently moored on Bolinas Lagoon at the end of Wharf Road in Bolinas. A tucked-away town just off Highway 1 in Marin County, Bolinas was *the* place to live an alternative lifestyle. The barge was just a two-minute walk to the beach. Primo location! Expensive piece of property, lavishly furnished. There were three staterooms; a large living room overlooking the water; a huge deck; and various bunks, nooks and crannies throughout the barge where one could lay out a sleeping bag and claim a small personal space. Eight strangers in all. I think I was given a stateroom because I was older than the rest of them and had to get up for work.

We were told we were not to use any of the equipment—water skis, a small skiff, fishing tackle, clam shovels and other necessities for living the good life at the beach. We were limited in another, more significant way: we had to move out on alternate weekends because the owner had reserved the use of the house for herself. That meant packing up most of our belongings and disappearing two weekends a month. What I owned at the time fit into my car so this was not a problem. I stayed with friends in San Francisco.

The organizer of this communal living endeavor, Audrey, was an accomplished con artist. It took us a while to realize we had all been conned, but by then we had already settled in. Audrey had recently arrived from Arkansas with one son. Her other three children were in foster care. She posed as a woman of wealth with a staff and extended family—nanny, accountant, chauffeur, maid, assorted relatives—and rented large properties in Marin County. I saw her once in her costume after she had returned from a meeting with the attorneys who managed these superior properties. She looked the part, dressed in her tasteful black suit; diamonds (fake); expensive shoes and matching handbag; cultured, polished speaking voice and manner. She knew how to negotiate with people at a high level in the San Francisco legal and financial world. She fooled them all, a skilled imposter.

She would re-rent the properties to people like me who wanted to live communally, charging double the rent she had negotiated with the property representatives. With four or five housing arrangements like ours, she was doing quite well financially. I heard about but never visited the twelve-bedroom estate near Dominican College filled with museum quality furniture.

I was working at *Rolling Stone* in San Francisco at the time and had to be at work at 8 a.m. I was the only one with a job. The others were living on unemployment, welfare or trust funds. They spent their days getting high and enjoying the sun and the waterbed on the deck.

Little house cleaning was ever done, so before the move-out weekends we had to vacuum the grit embedded in the long loops of elegant yellow and white wool carpet, gently clean with toothbrushes the grime on the arms of the silk upholstered chairs, and try to cover the scratches on the antique tables. Audrey would be there to make sure it was done right. She had her livelihood to protect. I always worked hard, resenting the others who melted away on those Fridays. Those who did show up would stand around looking helpless. I imagined they had grown up with a household staff or a mother who did everything for them. But I loved the elegance of the place and imagined myself the owner, so I scrubbed with Audrey.

We were a loose group. No meetings, no one in charge. I had bought my first ten-speed bicycle and parked it in the garage. The next day after work when I went to try it out, it wasn't there. Furious, I confronted my housemates. Jeff said, through a drug haze, "Oh, well, property is theft." I fumed my response: "What kind of Marxist bullshit is that?" Some anger is righteous anger. Mine was, and I used it. If my bike was not in the garage by the next evening I would call the police.

My beautiful white Peugeot bicycle was in the garage when I got home from work the next day. Since our tenancy on the barge was highly questionable, if not illegal, my threat was effective. Longtime residents of Bolinas didn't like hippies descending on their town, with their drugs, casual approach to sanitation, and no apparent means of support. The local postmistress was the self-appointed gatekeeper trying to stem the hippie migration to Bolinas by requiring absolute proof of a

115

local address in order to receive mail and, of course, checks. No one at our house wanted the police to come knocking or to have those precious unemployment checks interrupted.

Bolinas was on the circuit of roaming hippies in the sixties, along with places like Bali, Nepal, Thailand and India. One weekend that summer I counted seventeen strangers crashing at our house. There were no red wine stains or burn holes in the furniture from careless pot smokers, but I was uncomfortable, to say the least, to have that many strangers staying there. I was equally uneasy with my housemates who had stolen from my room a tee shirt, some towels, money, and a tab of window pane LSD, said to be the purest. Foolish me to mention it.

One evening late in the summer Audrey arrived at the house with her boyfriend and another man. The two had been released just that afternoon after twelve years in San Quentin. We weren't told their crimes and I didn't dare ask. I felt tense. They also seemed uneasy. Were they dangerous? Would they celebrate, get drunk and lose control? I tried not to stare at them for fear of antagonizing them. That was the evening I decided to move. I had been there three months.

I heard later that Audrey had become a producer of festivals and concerts in San Francisco. She had found another line of work, and I had satisfied my curiosity about communal living. We housemates didn't bond with each other. I can't even remember their names except for Jeff who drove an olive green Porsche and who was the victim of vandalism when someone poured sugar in his gas tank. I learned something important about myself—I don't like living communally, and I wouldn't like it even with friends.

I found emergency housing on San Pedro Road in San Rafael. Very recently it had been someone's dream house, overlooking San Francisco Bay. No nearby neighbors, spacious rooms, picture windows. I was told my sunny room would be available for only two months, since the house was condemned. That was perfect. The boat dock and low bluffs a short distance away were crumbling into the Bay and the house would soon be threatened. Almost empty of furnishings, the house felt sad and already abandoned even though there were four of us living there. I remember an eerie quiet and an odd but not unpleasant odor.

I dislike grime and spent several days scrubbing the many cabinet doors of the large kitchen. I was aware this was irrational, since I would be there barely long enough to use the kitchen. If the others noticed this odd behavior, they didn't say anything. At least the condemned house would die with a clean kitchen.

After I finished scrubbing the forlorn kitchen, I went house-hunting. Again, I found a notice on the Telegraph Avenue Co-op bulletin board for an opening in a group house in Oakland. Even though I had decided not to live communally, this was all I could afford at the time. When I left San Francisco I had a feeling I would eventually settle in Berkeley or Oakland. So, from San Francisco, to Marin and finally to the East Bay. I disregarded the words scrawled on the notice: "Nasty people."

But nice neighborhood! Sunny Hills Road in Crocker Highlands. Nice house; four bedrooms, large living room, dining room. A piano. The people seemed fine. A married couple and a single man. I moved in and then Bill, a recovering IBM computer scientist, arrived. He was Bill Two. Bill One, the original resident, taught self-awareness and led "human potential" seminars. He had to be a guy who had worked out his personal kinks and therefore easy to get along with. You know, self-aware, willing to talk things out.

We planned a big party, inviting everyone we knew. Saturday morning of party day we were all sitting at the dining room table when I said something to Bill One which made him very angry. He swung and slapped me. Never, ever had I been slapped. Bill Two immediately tried to intervene. Bill One and Two were hitting and shoving each other. It was bad, made worse by the fact that Bill One outweighed Bill Two by about seventy-five pounds. Cathy climbed onto the dining room table, the better to cheer on her husband, Bill One. I thought this was a terrible idea since she was five months pregnant. Chairs tipped over, the iron and ironing board in the corner crashed to the floor. I was afraid someone would pick up the iron and use it as a weapon. I could not believe what was happening. As I watched Bills One and Two, I noticed I could no longer see color. All color was gone from the room. Everything and everyone was black, white and gray. It wasn't until the fight was over that I regained color vision.

I knew I needed to make a strong statement to Bill One that his hitting me and fighting was absolutely unacceptable, so I called the police. They responded quickly, lectured us briefly, and left. Then I called my friends to tell them the party was off. One friend offered to take me out for dinner. I remember salting my food three or four times until I realized I couldn't taste anything.

"Nasty people." How did the writer of those words know? Had something like this happened before?

Bill Two and I became a couple and planned to move out together. Of course, there was no more "group" living. We barely spoke to Bill One and Cathy, bought our own food, ate separately. It took Bill and me another year to be ready to find another place to live. In that year we hung out mostly in my bedroom in the evenings when I practiced my guitar and Bill Two read. There were no more fights. I think this one scared everyone.

That was my last experiment in group living.

Bill Two and I lived together three years. Our relationship was falling apart, and he began dating other women while we were still living together. One Saturday evening as he was leaving, I threw a dill pickle at him. That clinched it. (How limp!)

I found my own apartment. Even though I was not in love with him, I had become attached enough so that I lost my appetite with the loss. I had never, ever lost my appetite, even when I was sick. For a week all I could eat was an ice cream sundae from Fenton's.

One Saturday afternoon my doorbell rang. It was the Oakland Public Health Department asking me if I knew Bill. Yes. Well, you need to be tested for gonorrhea. Whaaa? I called Bill who reluctantly confessed to having had a threesome with a couple who picked him up hitchhiking while he was on a trip to Florida. (Eeew!) He had picked up gonorrhea. Who was this piece of Limburger I had been living with? I didn't think he sounded guilty enough. Got my test and I was clear, and clear of him.

## Guru Farewell Party

I was invited to a late-evening farewell party in San Francisco for an Indian guru. The earlier part of the evening my date (name lost to history) and I attended the opening of a porno film made by Fredric Hobbs, a San Francisco artist. But first we had a light peyote cocktail to enhance our soft porn movie experience. All I remember about the film is the title, "Roseland," and the ending where the heroine, waving and smiling, rides off into space straddling a penis-shaped spaceship. Still high on peyote we drove round and round through the Mission before my addled date found the apartment where we would meet and then bid farewell to the guru.

The apartment was a plain, sparsely-furnished place. The small living room was packed with so many devotees we could hardly find floor space on which to sit. Buttocks to buttocks, we waited for the guru to appear. The longer we waited the stronger the hum of expectation became. As the hours went by the tension in the room became almost unbearable. I did not know this guru, one among many from India who found devoted followers in the sixties in the Bay Area. I learned that he had been denied an extension to his visa and was being deported. His sorrowing followers were there to say goodbye. Despite never having heard of this man, I was amazed to realize that I longed to see him, that I felt deep love for him, and that I ached knowing he was leaving. When he finally emerged, wearing the expected white robes and gray beard, my need to touch him was as strong as my need for oxygen. I sobbed as he walked by.

The logical reasons why I might be so affected by someone I didn't know at all (that is, the earlier peyote and the emotion in the room) don't satisfactorily explain my feelings of being transported into a sacred realm. I just knew I had been in the presence of a holy man. I am grateful to know they exist.

I went on the very first trip of Backroads Bicycle Tours of Berkeley in 1979.

I had met friends Linda and Tom in Berkeley, cycling enthusiasts who believed the sport had potential as a business. They would tap this potential by leading bicycle tours. Backroads had only two paying guests for their inaugural, five-day trip through Death Valley. Tom and Linda needed to appear established, so Linda asked if I would go with them to enlarge the group. I'd pay only for my food.

They were eager to impress: they cooked our breakfast, set out our lunch and cooked our dinner, which included wine. They used ceramic dishes and glass stemware. No paper plates here. They set up and took down our tents. We didn't have to lift a finger, not even with cleanup. This was five-star camping.

They kept close tabs on us from their van as we rode through Death Valley, essential given the geography, lack of water and high temperatures. Luckily, it was an unusually cool April, so no one was in danger of heat exhaustion. The days were windy and we often had to ride into a headwind. One night the wind blew so hard the tents collapsed, and the five of us spent the rest of the night huddled in the van, rocked by the wind as it howled around us.

We saw few tourists, but we did meet a friendly couple who had spent an entire day sitting in the sand dunes, transfixed as they watched the changing shapes, shadows, and colors of the dunes, their concentration enhanced with marijuana. This is still near the top of my bucket list.

Death Valley is a desert, and the only way to really see a desert is to get right out into it. I would leave my bike at the side of the road and walk out a short distance, sit down and see what I could find. My idea of a desert was from *Lawrence of Arabia*—empty expanses, nothing but sand. What I saw in Death Valley was the desert floor carpeted with tiny succulents in a myriad of shapes and colors. From the road, one wouldn't know they were there. This miniature world could be seen only if one were sitting down in it. There must have been critters residing there too, but I wasn't keen to meet them for fear of being bitten or stung, so I wouldn't stay long.

Furnace Creek is as its name suggests: the water in this shallow creek is warm and inviting. In that chilly April, I could have lain down and bathed in it but we had miles to go.

I went on two more Backroads tours, one through Glacier National Park and the other through Bryce and Zion and on to the north rim of the Grand Canyon. On that trip I rode my personal one-day best: one hundred and five miles.

Backroads couldn't keep up the inaugural level of service as the business grew. We had to put up our own tents and help with meal preparation and cleanup. No more ceramic plates or glass stemware. Today, Backroads is a phenomenally successful company which leads tours all over the world. Their bike tours average about six hundred dollars a day; my Death Valley trip was free. I do have a residual unpleasant taste about Backroads. I don't know the whole story, but I know Tom and Linda's parting was not a cordial one.

If I can't wholeheartedly recommend a Backroads tour, I can recommend a trip through Death Valley on any conveyance—haunting, bizarre, spiritual. Unforgettable, like nowhere else on earth.

## SUNDAY MORNING IN THE HAIGHT

In 1967, Sister Sharon was visiting me in San Francisco and I suggested she might like to check out the Haight. See the "hippies," a catch-all but derisive term for students, musicians, wanderers and seekers in the sixties.

We strolled past the tee shirt and head shops, closed that quiet Sunday morning. Unusually quiet. Then people began to appear on the street, more and more of them, forming a large crowd. We had stumbled into the middle of a confrontation between the hippies of the Haight and the TAC Squad (police in riot gear). The Haight Street mass moved slowly toward the TAC Squad. The Squad would move back and then advance. Opposing forces threatening and then retreating, threatening and retreating, keeping a decent distance from each other. I could feel the tension. The air was full of static electricity. Then things got ugly. I had not noticed people on rooftops. They began throwing glass bottles, shattering them in the street. People started running. I remember feeling the wind created by people running by. We were scared, huddled in a doorway of a shop wondering what to do when a policeman appeared. It was clear we were not one of the demonstrators. He told us we should get out of there and escorted us away from the crowd.

We were accidental eye witnesses to one of the many violent encounters between the San Francisco police and hippies in the sixties.

## SYNCHRONICITY OR JUST UNEXPLAINABLE WEIRDNESS?

I had just arrived home from work when my roommate and her boyfriend invited me to attend a séance with them. They were leaving right away so I dropped everything and went with them. They had heard about a Jamaican man in town briefly who was holding séances in the basement of a house in the Haight. We were late and the man was talking, apparently already in a trance. About a dozen people sat in rows of folding chairs. We paid our ten dollars and found seats. The Jamaican was seated on a low platform with a small spotlight on him, the only light in the room. His eyes were closed. I didn't know the protocol at a séance or whether questions had been invited before we arrived, so I just watched and listened. He spoke at length. I couldn't make out what he was saying. Then I heard him say, "I'm getting something about Agnes and July in Portland." I froze. That was my mother's name, and I was going to Portland in July. I didn't know whether to feel excited or alarmed so I was still, hoping for more. That's all there was, and he went on to something else. We sat for a bit longer, and then we left. When I told Gail and Arnie that I had been spoken to at the seance, they just shrugged as though it was insignificant. It wasn't to me. To this day I wonder what it meant.

Another synchronous event: Much later I was living with Bill. Not happy. I could not forget a Portland man whom I loved. One sunny Saturday morning I got up early, sat in the bean bag chair in the living room and cried. When Bill got up I told him I could not get Portland man out of my mind. I needed to go to Portland to find out once and for all whether we had a relationship and whether I should move there.

Several hours later the phone rang. It was a woman from Ira Progoff's institute in New York. Dr. Progoff had studied with Carl Jung in Switzerland for several years and had developed his own approach to Jungian ideas. He traveled around the country staging in-depth journal-writing workshops. I had assisted them with the one he did in Oakland. They had scheduled one at Marylhurst College in Portland and wanted me to work for them again since I had done such a good job. They would pay my airfare.

I might not have been so eager to go if I hadn't had another agenda. I worked the workshop and then met with Portland man who said if I moved to Portland I would not be seeing much of him. Thank you Ira Progoff for helping me solve that long, painful dilemma.

In my first week working at *Rolling Stone* magazine in 1971, my easy life ended and I became a meat-eater again. I had been living on unemployment benefits for months and had become a vegetarian. Stir fry of brown rice, sunflower seeds, veggies and tamari was the dish of the day among hippies. I loved it. Healthy and affordable, I ate it every night.

My unemployment insurance had run out, and I began my job search further into the counterculture with an interview as assistant to Bill Graham, the rock concert promoter. I felt uneasy during the interview with Bill Graham's business manager. I didn't get the job. I felt relieved. Something about the way he was checking me out during the interview. Something about the long sofa in the office. I knew there was quite a bit of truth to the notion that the music business was about sex, drugs, and rock and roll. Having grown up in a small blue-collar town, I would have felt more at ease working with longshoremen than with rock musicians.

Soon after, I found a job as assistant to the editor of the newly formed book division of *Rolling Stone—Straight Arrow Books*. With a liberal arts degree, publishing was a better fit for me than music. I think organizations like these were interested in me because I was both hip and competent. I looked the part with my long hair and round, gray-tinted granny glasses. And I had valuable experience as a legal secretary. I could type 130 words a minute and could spell.

*Rolling Stone*'s publisher, Jann Wenner, had hired Alan Rinzler, whom he introduced as the "boy wonder" of Manhattan publishing, to head up *Straight Arrow Books*. Alan had a reputation for recognizing good, unpublished writers with something important to say.

I soon found how wrong was my preconceived idea that *Rolling Stone* would be a laid back place to work. Alan walked fast, talked fast, worked fast. Jann Wenner himself might just as well have worn roller skates he moved so quickly through the office. They were vast—the top floor of a warehouse south of Market. Lots of exposed wood, polished floors, an occasional Oriental rug. The receptionist's pet Sheltie never missed a day.

Alan Rinzler today has a successful career in Berkeley as a book editor. His clients have included Toni Morrison, Tom Robbins, Robert Ludlum, Andy Warhol, Hunter S. Thompson and Shirley MacLaine. And my friend Jan Stites. He is still a "boy wonder," only older.

Everyone was so busy at *Rolling Stone* there was little time for get-acquainted conversations, so I didn't make any friends there. It was hectic, and I needed a hamburger for lunch my first day, breaking my vegetarian regimen. I was living in the communal house in Bolinas at the time, an hour's drive into the city. I had to be at work at eight in the morning. I found a woman to commute with me. To ease the daily ordeal driving back home over Mt. Tamalpais we would drink sherry directly from the bottle. Reckless days!

130

Part of my job was to review submitted manuscripts, most of which seemed to have been conceived in a drug haze, hand-written on scraps of paper, poor grammar and spelling, some essentially unreadable. Alan decided to publish a primer about making your own clothes, extending the do-it-yourself ethos of the sixties. Many of us made our own candles, our own yogurt, our own macramé plant hangers. I was an accomplished seamstress, having taught myself to sew as a kid, so I was unimpressed with the flour-sack designs. I didn't say anything, deferring to him to know what would sell. I don't recall how well the book did.

I was given the task of planning a party to launch the book. My boss made it clear this was my baby. He wouldn't be there. I was on my own. I rented the venue, did the advertising, arranged for the keg of beer and food, and hired Dan Hicks and his Hot Licks. The band showed up over two hours late. I fretted about how to entertain the guests. Was I supposed to come up with some kind of impromptu entertainment to keep them interested? I had no ideas and certainly was not a performer myself. We were running out of food and beer. But most guests waited it out and stayed. My original hunches were right. I would not have been comfortable working in the music business.

Alan and I were not a good fit, and I was there only four months. There really wasn't much work to do. I was intimidated by him with his stellar New York reputation and his Harvard degree. I feared he would criticize my ideas, so I avoided him as much as possible, although we had adjoining offices. Now I realize he needed a confident assistant, and my insecurity prevented me from giving him what he needed.

I read a recent interview with him, and it was clear that I was not in on anything that was going on at *Rolling Stone* at the time. Perhaps if I had been more comfortable, I would have heard some of the really interesting gossip about famous writers, musicians, and artists who filtered through; about the organizational problems; about Jann Wenner's changeability; and about the precarious financial state of *Rolling Stone* in the early days. But at this time I was deep into my own psychotherapy and couldn't take in anyone else's disorganization and financial insecurity.

## CHICKEN COOP BOYFRIEND

In 1972 I had a boyfriend who lived in a chicken coop in Petaluma. When chickens lived in it, there had been enough space for hundreds of them. Eric hung his clothes on the former roosts. He had a makeshift kitchen at one end, a woodshop at the other. He used an eight-foot ladder to reach his bunk bed, built high up just under the ceiling. I don't know why it was built so high. Did foxes still come into the coop at night hunting for chickens?

I met Eric through a singles ad. His unusual address was interesting enough but what really captivated me was that he was a woodworker. I like men who have calluses on their hands, who can build things. Later I learned he was a sculptor as well. Even better. He would come to my apartment in San Francisco or I would go to his chicken coop in Petaluma. Eric was comfortable in the chicken coop. I was not. It was a dusty place and he was usually floured with sawdust from his woodworking as well as remnant chicken dust from the coop. He was a gifted woodworker, employed part time as a boat builder in Marin. His income was minimal. He was separated from his wife and had to help support her and their four children. A low-rent chicken coop was all he could afford. I disliked staying overnight there. Dust sifted down from the rafters and the sheets were always gritty.

One day he led me to a corner of the coop where a form was covered by a tarp. Shyly, he carefully removed the cover and there stood a rocking horse.

He had worked on it for an entire year, beginning with laminating the wood to form a block large enough to carve into a rocking horse. The head and body were realistically sculpted and smoothly sanded, the bristly, kinky mane and tail of untwisted sisal rope. The rocking horse with its alert brown eyes was as perfect as a museum piece. He planned to build three more, one for each of his children. His family had returned to their home in Hawaii; a trial separation. Perhaps they had moved to Northern California to try to save their marriage. I learned of his family only after we started dating. When he worked through some personal issues, he planned to reconcile and rejoin them. Eventually, I heard his story. He had married young and had had four children quickly. Restless and unhappy, he felt he needed to date a lot of women. He knew he had missed out on an important time in life, his twenties, when one typically has a number of partners. Now he was a troubled, discouraged person. Although trying to turn back the clock, he knew he could not and might even lose his family.

One weekend at dusk we drove through ranchland in Sonoma owned by a friend and up a remote mountaintop where we unrolled our sleeping bags, swallowed LSD, and waited for a celestial trip flying through the cosmos, dodging meteors, visiting stars, maybe seeing God. If our expectations hadn't been so high we could have enjoyed sleeping out in this spectacular private preserve, closer to the stars than Eric's bunk bed was to the ceiling of the coop. I didn't have a grand cosmic adventure, and Eric couldn't retrieve his twenties.

After only a few months of seeing Eric, he was ready to rejoin his family, and he came to San Francisco to say goodbye. He had only one rocking horse to take to his children, not four.

He handed me a white gift box. It was heavy for its size. Inside was a wood sculpture, as smooth as the real thing and as beautifully sculpted as the rocking horse. It was a life-size erect penis on a base of two balls. I had no words. I looked at him in confusion. He was not smiling. Surely he did not mean for me to *use* it, anatomically speaking. I thought, maybe, bookend, but it was not heavy enough.

I didn't know what the appropriate words of thanks were for such an unusual memento. I think he was thanking me for being in his life at a difficult time and asking me to remember him. He didn't know how memorable he was, and I did not know that I had really meant something to him. The sculpted penis expressed words he could not say.

I kept it for several years, but it was an awkward thing to have around. With mixed feelings, I put it in the trash.

I have a snapshot of me posing on a beach in Acapulco in a red and white polka dot bikini. As I was walking on the beach in that bikini, I met a tall, handsome, tanned and trim American guy who said he was a ski instructor at Vail and invited me to come to Vail next winter. I could stay at his condo. I could bring a friend. I said I'd love to.

Harry was a model of your glossy ski magazine's lanky, self-confident ski instructor accustomed to having women fall all over him. Glamorous guys didn't usually notice me. I wasn't gorgeous. I was puzzled by his invitation and a bit suspicious. Was this just one of those air kiss invitations—not juicy, not real? But I really wanted to go to Vail, and when ski season came I ignored my earlier doubts and called Harry to tell him I'd like to take him up on his offer. We had not been in touch since Acapulco. Neither one of us had written down phone numbers at the beach. I eventually found his number in information. I hoped he remembered me. I told him I was bringing a friend. I could not imagine staying at his place for a week without a female companion.

Fine, fine, he said and told me how to find his place and if he wasn't there he would hide a key. Vail was a new but already fashionable ski destination. I invited friend Gail who was glad to have a chance to ski Vail. I was a beginner but she was an accomplished skier who wanted to try Vail's famous powder. And I wanted to impress her with my knowing a real Vail ski instructor.

Harry was there when we arrived. He seemed distracted and rushed. He showed us our room and then left abruptly. Gail and I looked at each other. Not such a good start. We didn't see him that evening or the next morning. Not at lunch or after skiing the next day. It was obvious we were not welcome. But it was worse to have Gail see how I had advocated for this trip based on nothing more than a questionable invitation from a stranger on a Mexican beach.

We found a hotel room, returned for our stuff, left Harry a note and moved out. I don't know what Gail thought of me for having gotten her into this mess. Neither of us had planned on the considerable expense of paying for a hotel room.

The rest of the week was a blur. I was numb, not because of the cold but from mortification. I had thought that I would at least spend some time with Harry even if it did not become a romance. I wanted to go home but Gail was enjoying herself. She had met Frank, another instructor, and spent all her time with him. I dragged myself through the week. I took classes each day, and each day I had to repeat the beginner's class. Another humiliation. As a novice I found it impossible to ski in knee-deep powder. I needed to see my skis. In the evenings, I sat by myself at the bar, feeling miserable and conspicuous in my red hand-knit ski sweater. No one seemed to notice me or came to talk to me. I felt like lead. No wonder I couldn't ski.

I never did see Harry. He was keeping himself scarce.

I survived the humiliation and went on two more ski weeks the following two ski seasons, one at Aspen and one at Sun Valley. Aspen was also a skiing disaster. My instructor was interested only in picking up women, not in teaching us how to ski moguls. It was beyond my ability to ski them correctly by making quick turns in the little valleys between mounds. I just skied over them, stalling at the top with my skis dangling in midair. This week was better socially. Friend Kristin and I had a good time on the long train trip from Berkeley to Denver. She was good at flirting, and we found two guys who were good at *apres-ski*, and we spent the week together at Aspen.

The best ski instructors were at Sun Valley, and I began to get the hang of it. I don't remember much socializing, but the outdoor hot tub was heavenly after skiing hard all day.

A few weeks after returning from Sun Valley I went to Squaw Valley and—miracle—I could ski. Everything came together. I could feel it. I got the rhythm. I could let myself hang way forward in my boots facing downhill. I could without fear shift my weight to my downhill ski, trusting that the uphill edge would hold me from slipping down the steep slope. I could begin a turn at just the right moment, using my pole to lift and shift my weight over both skis to carve a beautiful, smooth arc, back and forth across my favorite runs called Siberia and Shirley Lake.

The highlight of my skiing career came at the end of that season when I skied a few runs with the Ski

Patrol guys whose cabin I stayed in. How I came to stay in that award-winning cabin especially built for the 1960s Olympics I don't remember. I was young and reasonably attractive, and glamorous opportunities just seemed to drop in my lap. The ski patrol guys were experts and I was far from it, but on the moderate runs I could keep up with them. And with no thanks at all to you, Harry of Vail.

Those of us exploring an "alternative" lifestyle had discovered how easy it was to claim government benefits like unemployment, food stamps, Medicaid and even SSI disability. During periods of unemployment almost everyone I knew got some payment or other. It was us against "the system." I think the idea was to overwhelm and then sink it. I wasn't interested in toppling the government and reordering society. I just wanted some of the goodies, so I applied for Medicaid to supplement my unemployment benefits.

When I heard about a psychiatrist who practiced Rolfing and accepted Medicaid I made an appointment. One more approach to self-realization, this time through the muscles. It was known to be terribly painful. Ida Rolf had devised a method of torture by applying intense pressure, slowly and forcefully, to major muscles to break down the fascia. Think of an orange, those little globules containing the juice. That's what fascia looks like. A good Rolfer skipped no body parts—inside the mouth, the groin, the feet. Ten sessions. This would supposedly take one to a higher level of consciousness.

Dr. X lived in the Montclair hills of Oakland and had a lovely, large office on the lower level of his house. There was no conversation corner in his office for talk therapy, but there was an examining table and a large cabinet containing a pharmacy. Apparently Dr. X had found Rolfing more rewarding than psychoanalysis.

I climbed onto the table and prepared for the ordeal. Dr. X began with my thighs. I was surprised at how little it hurt. I began to be suspicious that he was not a legitimate Rolfer. By the third session I knew it and decided to relax and enjoy myself. The treatments were more like a firm massage than a tenderizing and reordering of my very being which, according to Ida Rolf, was constricted within my unsoftened muscular fascia. Dr. X never did work the inside of my mouth or my groin. I was relieved. I thought perhaps I had already reached enlightenment, since Dr. X didn't seem to soften anything anywhere. As we passed the recommended tenth session, I knew he was running a scam, just as I was. We were complicit in duping the system.

About the twelfth session he asked me if I would like to try muscle-testing. Oh, sure. What was it? He told me to raise my arm and then dropped several tablets from a bottle in his pharmacy onto my navel. Could he push my arm down? Yes. More tablets from a different bottle landed on my navel. Could he push my arm down? Yes. When there was a small pyramid of pills he had constructed on my navel, finally he could not push my arm down. That's the number of tablets I would take daily for strength.

I left with a bag of a dozen bottles and a very large bill. Medicaid didn't cover muscle-testing.

The first several days the supplements filled me so that I had no room for food. I was zooming with energy. Then the effect wore off and I got tired of swallowing pills instead of eating.

I went back for a few more sessions, about sixteen in all, and Dr. X pronounced me Rolfed. I left, with no more illumination than before. The remainder of the pills landed in the trash.

## White Light

It was a normal, summer Saturday morning and I was on the streetcar riding down Market Street in San Francisco headed for the East Bay Terminal to visit Kristin and Allen who had moved from San Francisco to the Glenview neighborhood in Oakland. I don't remember now, but it must have been during a time when I was experimenting regularly with hallucinogens and marijuana.

On the streetcar, I began to feel a little strange, like I might pass out. All of a sudden I could not see. I saw nothing except a bright, white light. No buildings, no cars, no people. No nothing except whiteness. I remember how clearly I knew what to do. How surprised I was to recognize what I needed. I said very softly to the woman sitting next to me, "I'm having some difficulty, not feeling well, and I wonder if I might hold your hand until I feel better. I need to close my eyes and have you tell me where we are." She took my hand and I grasped hers, trying not to squeeze too hard. She named the streets as we rolled by—Dolores, Guerrero, Valencia. I was afraid, but I didn't think there was anything seriously wrong with me. I told myself this was temporary. Above all, I knew I needed to stay calm. I focused on her voice, the street names. Gradually the frightening feelings began to recede. When we reached Van Ness I felt better and opened my eyes. My sight had returned to normal. The white light was gone and I could see the other passengers, passing cars, buildings. I could let go of the stranger's hand. I told her what had been happening to me and thanked her. I wanted to hug her in gratitude but did not. I didn't think to ask her name.

I can't explain why it happened. Maybe it was a drug reaction. Perhaps anxiety. But it scared me enough that I decided to stop experimenting.

# AM I THERE YET?
# (Therapy to Grad School to Private Practice)

I started therapy in San Francisco soon after my LSD experiences. I was thirty-two and depressed since age fourteen, but I didn't call it that. I called it unhappy, angry and lacking self-confidence.

I had no direction to my life, no career ideas. Only vague dreams. Get married, I suppose, but I skipped over the part of meeting someone and falling in love. I moved almost once a year and changed undemanding clerical jobs as often. I wore jeans and lots of little silver rings on my fingers. All my energy went into pretending everything was all right, concealing from myself and others how unhappy I was. Afraid I would be found out if anyone got too close. Even though I was lonely, I made sure no one did get too close.

My friends Kristin and Allen were in a therapy group together. Kristin was one of the original members of our self-proclaimed Green Street Gang in San Francisco, and Allen was her new boyfriend. She seemed happier. I saw her developing a presence and self-confidence that said, "Take me seriously. I am someone to listen to." Her transformation from a diffident and self-effacing person was remarkable. They were leaving me behind. I knew I was lost but did not have the word for it at the time. I wanted Kristin's self-confidence. I knew what I had to do.

Full of dread, I made an appointment at a counseling center I found in the Yellow Pages. I climbed the steps of the Sacramento Street Victorian, wishing I could dissolve into the acidic humiliation I felt. No trap door opened to allow me to escape. As I sat in the crowded waiting room, I imagined everyone knew why I was there—something was wrong with me. During the intake interview, I was surprised to be crying so hard I couldn't answer the woman's questions. She made an appointment for me with a psychologist.

I'm sure he had the biggest and best office in the building with its fireplace, built-in bookcases, and comfortable leather furniture. In my mind that meant he saw only the sickest people, confirming there was *really* something wrong with me. If there weren't, I would be seeing a social worker in a smaller office. I paid for the therapy myself. I didn't think to ask whether my insurance at work covered it. I think the fee was $25 an hour.

I began weekly Monday meetings. I dreaded hearing Dr. Weisenfeld coming down the stairs to meet me. I dragged myself behind him up the steep stairs and long hallway to his office. He sat patiently waiting for me to start. My always having to speak first was the most excruciating part of the session. I felt cornered, scrutinized, simply because he was looking at me. I didn't know what to talk about. Mostly I just cried. It was like having to pry open a heavy, iron door tightly closed since early childhood. I was now being asked to undo the family prohibition against expressing any painful or angry feelings. The doctor would say a few words at the end of the hour and I would leave.

He was a Jungian analyst, which meant dreams. As a good, dutiful patient, I had lots of them. I had one the night before my first appointment. Right on time. My dream: I was clinging for dear life to the top of the flagpole in the yard of my childhood home swaying wildly in a terrible storm. He said it meant that I had been deeply injured. His words were like an arrow aimed straight into the center of my being. He recognized something that neither I nor anyone had ever understood.

I couldn't stop crying but I felt something loosening inside. I can't say I felt good, but I knew something important had happened to me. I would go back. I didn't know what the injury was; that took many therapy hours to understand.

I had a series of dreams about the red Volkswagen I owned at the time. In one, the doors fell off. In others, it was stuck in sand or mud up to the fenders. My dreams confirmed how stuck I felt, just like my Volkswagen.

I dreaded the sessions. When he suggested we meet twice a week, my dread was doubled. Now it was not just Monday, but Thursday, too. My boss at the public relations firm, where I had the mind-numbing job of duplicating press releases and stuffing envelopes, let me leave work early for my five o'clock appointments. I was working so hard in therapy dragging out years of hurt that I could not have handled a more demanding job. Some days after my appointment all I could do was crawl into bed without dinner, emotionally and physically exhausted. It was the hardest work I have ever done.

I cried in every session for two years. Very little in my childhood could account for all that pain. No dramatic events like overt abuse or neglect. Just that time when I yelled and swore at Mrs. Holmes and lost my friends. Being replaced by a younger, more loved sibling? Possibly. There was clearly something vital missing for which I was grieving. I know what it was, but it seems inadequate to explain the magnitude of the pain I felt. Simply put, as I was growing up my mother could not give me the emotional closeness, warmth and understanding I needed. She had not received enough, and she didn't have it to give.

I could never meet Dr. Weisenfeld's gaze. One day after I had taken LSD again, I looked him straight in the eye as I talked. He commented and I brushed it off as no big deal. I still couldn't be honest with myself or with him. Then I got stuck and couldn't think of a thing to talk about. We sat in silence for many uncomfortable sessions. He had me sit in his chair to see if symbolically altering the power dynamics would loosen me up. It did not.

I decided to stop therapy with him not long after I had the following dream:

I'm in an empty house. It's night. No curtains on the window. I see Dr. Weisenfeld through the window trying to get in. I look around, desperate for something to protect myself. I grab a coat hanger from the closet and hold it like a sword.

When I told the doctor he made a small sound of surprise. He was a fine professional, not revealing his reactions, but this one he could not conceal.

I don't know what I was afraid of, but the message in the dream was clear: after more than three years I needed to move on. I had many more years of therapy, but the time with Dr. Weisenfeld was the most profound. I began to come alive in the work I did with him. I was transformed from being a stiff, made-up person to someone who could trust her own thoughts and feelings. I cried away a lot of my pretenses and made a good start toward recovering my real self. A priceless gift. Many years later when I was gathering references for graduate school I called him. I told him the work we did together saved my life.

## The Wrong Therapy Group

I next went from the painstaking, slow work of Jungian analysis to group therapy. I wanted to work with the same therapist Kristin and Allen had been seeing. The doctor really made me work to get into his group. I left three phone messages before he returned my call. When he did, he questioned my intentions. He was not sure he would let me into the group. I felt intimidated, wary. But I went ahead and joined when there was an opening.

Bob never had us call him Dr. Z____. He was just Bob. This informality didn't relax me. Bob wasn't really informal. He was scary. He glared and peered with suspicion; he was impatient.

Bob had trained under Eric Berne, author of *Games People Play*. I wondered why games were never mentioned. One member of our group would occasionally intone, "no foundation," which words themselves seemed to have no foundation. He would say them into the air, but I always thought he meant them for me. I assumed he thought I was dishonest. I was. I could not admit how afraid I was.

I didn't understand what I was supposed to do in the therapy group, having been given no introduction or instructions. As the group had been meeting for some time, I felt as though I had walked into the middle of a conversation. I didn't know how to get into the conversation. I always felt a sense of dread but assumed I was supposed to feel uncomfortable so I kept at it.

Three times a year we would go on marathons, weekend retreats where we were to work on our "projects." We met Friday evening through Sunday noon at a lodge in the Santa Cruz Mountains. The main room was paneled in dark wood, rustic and comfortable. We lounged on big pillows on the floor. There was even a cooler of beer and soda in the middle of the room. We could help ourselves but you can be sure someone kept a careful tally of who drank what.

"Projects" were commitments for change we had agreed upon in the weekly meetings prior to the marathons. For example: "Be good to myself," or "Speak my mind," or "Have more fun." They sound straightforward enough, but how does one go about purposely having fun under scrutiny and pressure?

I can't remember what my first project was, but the marathon went smoothly. I didn't do much of anything, for which I was praised as doing very well. I was puzzled but pleased. Bob said that dire things awaited you if you did not "graduate" from the group, and the only way to graduate was to complete your projects at the marathons.

When it was time for my third marathon, I couldn't think of a project. Bob suggested one: "Fix your mouth." Fix my mouth? What kind of therapy was this? I accepted the project but didn't have a clue what it meant. I was more uneasy than ever. At the marathon, I began working to "fix my mouth" by trying different kinds of smiles. I would twist my lips into different shapes, let them droop, let them pout. When the members voted that I had not "fixed my mouth," I was sent from the room. It was my job to try to rejoin the group. I knew this was the first step before expulsion from the marathon, leading to eventual expulsion from the therapy group itself. Desperate, I tried different shades of lipstick applied in different shapes. Each time I reentered the room to present my latest attempt to fix my mouth, I would be sent out again. After several of these humiliating reentries I gathered my things and left. At least I was the one making the decision. I wasn't going to let them humiliate me any longer.

Scared and angry, I drove home. I tried to make sense out of the colossal mismatch between the triviality of my assigned project and the awful, predicted consequences of ostracism. I was wretched.

In retrospect, trying to fix my mouth had to be pretty funny stuff. No one dared laugh at my attempts, however, because Bob warned members not to laugh at the others working on their projects.

Nothing was said about the marathon the following week at group, but there was a pronounced coldness in the room. The coolness continued and I persisted for another few miserable months. Then I quit. Bob predicted that if you left the group without his blessing, you would live a failed, dried up life and calamitous things would probably happen.

And a terrible thing did happen not long after I left. I had been to a big party with wine and marijuana on Saturday night. I was hung over on Sunday. That evening I drove to San Francisco to pick up a car-less friend and take her back to the communal house I had moved into in Oakland where we would have supper with a small group of friends. We had a bit of wine and a bit of marijuana and played music and sang. Then I drove her back to San Francisco.

On the way home and after I had dropped her off I fell asleep at the wheel on the Oakland side of the Bay Bridge. I woke to blinking dashboard lights. I had crashed into the concrete center divider. My seat belt had restrained me but I had bruised my knees. When the police arrived, I asked them for a ride home and they reluctantly agreed. This was not usually done. I was given a citation for "inattention." No sobriety test was given. With one loan payment to go, my car was totaled.

I was surprised by my reaction to the accident. I stayed home from work for four days and slept almost continuously. I couldn't stay awake, sleeping twenty hours every day.

I associated this accident with Bob's prediction of catastrophe. It was a curse, actually. In a way, the accident was fortuitous: I would not wonder the rest of my life when the predicted disaster would happen. I do question whether Bob's words had something to do with my accident. Perhaps I was tempting "fate," behaving with supreme recklessness and disregard for my safety.

Ram Das (Richard Alpert, a personal and professional associate of Timothy Leary at Harvard) wrote about the negative influence on him of a false teacher, and even after years of rigorous self-examination with his guru in India, he didn't see it coming. Bob was my false teacher. He was a bully. His methods were harmful to me. After that I vowed

I would never again allow anyone to exert that much power over me.

It wasn't until recently that I understood what "fix my mouth" meant. It came in a flash one morning as I was applying my makeup. I don't have full lips or a clean lip line. My lips are flat and rather narrow. I think Bob wanted me to know that sometimes I purse my lips, looking prim and severe. Of course, I would look prim and severe, given how tense I was around him. The irony is that a relaxed mouth comes from within, not from without, and my most valuable lesson was that in the beginning when Bob did not call back sooner I should have heeded my internal warnings and found a different therapist, one with whom I could feel safe.

I continued with more therapy. All in all, adding up encounter groups, individual and group therapy, and miscellaneous bodywork, I worked at it for about twenty-two years. I might have stayed a smidgen too long. When my practice took off I didn't need the support any longer and I stopped.

## Just Keep Sitting

Not long after the debacle with the wrong therapy group, I discovered Spirit Rock Buddhist meditation center in Woodacre in Marin County. I attended several day-long retreats. Then I decided to try a longer one. I found a teacher in San Jose and signed on for a thirty-day retreat, sight unseen. I was not working at the time and $400 was a lot of money, but I was keenly interested in intensive meditation. My life wasn't going very well with no career and no loving relationship, and I thought meditation would give me some answers.

We stayed at our teacher Sujata's home across the street from a quiet city park. He was an American who had been given the name (meaning "of noble birth") by his Buddhist teacher. The mahogany woodwork, arched doorways, and stained glass windows suggested wealth. On the grounds were a rose garden, fish pond, and several tiny cottages. The home had been given to Sujata by a student as a gift of gratitude.

Sujata told us that he could not decide whether he wanted to be a rock musician or study Vipassana Buddhism. I don't know how he narrowed his choice in this unlikely pairing. He chose the latter and spent ten years meditating in Ceylon, which he claimed was the original site of the Buddha's enlightenment. In his plain white monk's pajamas, Sujata was as tall and sinewy as Mick Jagger. When he played his guitar and sang for us in the evening, I could hear he might have succeeded at rock and roll too.

There were eight of us gathered in the new, light-filled meditation hall behind Sujata's house. A serene, soothing space. We were to observe silence at all times and have no eye contact with other students, so I have no idea who was there. The schedule: wakeup at five, an hour of meditation, breakfast, meditation, midday meal, a period of work, meditation, evening dharma talk with Sujata, meditation, evening tea, meditation, bedtime whenever we wished. We could do sitting or walking meditation anywhere in the hall and on the grounds. I looked forward to breakfast as the best time of day with its choice of five crunchy cereals and toppings of nuts, wheat germ, yogurt, fruit, and banana chips. It was our most sumptuous meal of the day. Our midday meal was forgettable— soup, rice, vegetables, bread.

Our only instruction was to watch our breath as we meditated. If it helped to focus, we could think "breathing in, breathing out." Walking meditation was "lifting, stepping, placing." Eating was "scooping, lifting, chewing, chewing, swallowing." The goal was to stay in the present moment by observing every thought, every minute action. It was hard work.

But it was not unrelieved repetition. During the evening dharma talks, Sujata would ask us how our practice was going, what we were experiencing, and then tell us something about his own experiences. According to this particular school of Vipassana Buddhism, there are four levels of enlightenment. He had achieved the first level. One who has achieved the fourth level is known as an arahat, so supremely enlightened that if his arm were chopped off he would feel no pain. So said Sujata.

My retreat was twice interrupted when I had to drive to Oakland to pick up my unemployment checks. I was instructed to describe to myself exactly what I was doing to stay in the present moment—driving, braking, steering, etc. Back problems from riding a runaway horse as a teen also interrupted my meditation, so I alternated periods of sitting with yoga.

One night was different. At the dharma talk that evening, Sujata told us that in many Asian countries a monk would go to a morgue to meditate on decomposing bodies to loosen his attachment to his physical body. (Attachment or desire is one of the five hindrances to staying in the present moment, along with boredom, anger, restlessness and doubt.) Sujata wished he could provide his own students with that opportunity. He envisioned a kind of Snow White glass coffin with a vent for escaping gases to satisfy the health authorities. I suspect this was only half in jest. We discussed our attachment to our bodies, which allow us to exist on the physical plane but which are just heavy things we have to drag around.

That evening as I was arranging myself into a comfortable position in my sleeping bag on the floor of the little cottage, I realized I could not move. The "I" that is me was a little blue flame deep inside my body, something like the pilot light of a gas stove. This heavy body that I drag around had trapped me inside. Now what do I do? Then I fell asleep.

That was the only time I have felt completely separate from my body.

I couldn't wait to tell Sujata about this at dharma talk the next evening. All he said was, "Just keep sitting." That's all? This fantastic thing had happened to me, and all I got was a deflating, "Just keep sitting."

My limit was only an hour of sitting meditation, but one evening after tea I sat down and sat, and sat, and sat. For about four hours. No pain. Finally, I got it. This must be "it"—the enlightenment I was looking for, although I certainly could not admit that to myself. Too pretentious. Disappointed, I was in pain again the next day. And again Sujata said, "Just keep sitting." Another time as I was meditating I began to cry but the tears were coming from only one eye. I didn't bother to tell Sujata. At the end of the retreat I learned that one man had managed to sit for twenty-two hours straight. I can't imagine how he achieved this.

I have meditated very little since the retreat. Recently, I had an ah-ha moment: talking about a past experience, whether it happened yesterday or years ago, takes one out of the present moment. Staying in the present moment is the essence of the awakened state. So when I told Sujata about being trapped in my body, I was recalling a past experience. That's why he said, "Just keep sitting." Thirty years later I got it.

Meditation practice is excellent training for therapists. At the time of the retreat I didn't know that's what was calling me, but some part of me must have known. At the retreat I learned the peace of quieting my mind and stilling my body. I learned there are hidden and surprising aspects to the human mind. I learned I didn't have to "do,' I could just "be."

First, some true confessions about work.

One spring morning NPR interviewed the new chief of the National Hurricane Center about the advent of hurricane season in June. He said he knew from the time he was three years old he wanted to study hurricanes. I was struck by the difference between him and me. It took me many years to find my calling. I have a secret resumé no prospective employer ever saw, listing the nineteen jobs I had in twenty years between college and graduate school.

Several jobs I kept only a few days. One was at a medical center in San Francisco where two cardiac specialists did everything short of heart transplants. On my second day as I was being shown around the hospital, we came upon a patient having a "sinking spell." Her face was a ghastly gray. There were a dozen doctors and nurses around her bed, pounding on her chest and performing other frantic maneuvers to resuscitate her. No one noticed me, of course, as I slid to the floor, trying not to faint. Without a word to anyone, I slipped away and out the door, never to return. I am ashamed to this day I left the way I did, but I couldn't face my employers because I didn't want to be persuaded to stay. It was clear to me I did not belong in physical medicine.

I had two different jobs at UC Berkeley, one for some genius or other who at twenty-three was the youngest person ever to earn a Berkeley doctorate. This was 1978; perhaps that record has since been surpassed. He had a research grant to study how children spent their time. I don't know where the children were. I never saw any. I had nothing to do. The office was quiet and dark. There was no one around except his secretary who also seemed to have little to do. For nine months I worked there half-time, filling those tedious four hours with an extended lunch.

My second job at UC Berkeley was in the newly established professional school of public policy. It was rolling in dough. Unlike my first UC job, the place was a beehive, with many support staff coming and going. However, like the first job, most seemed to have hardly anything to do either. With my nonexistent workload, I could take several hours for lunch exploring the Berkeley hills without being missed. One secretary left four afternoons a week to see her analyst. The professors would hold elaborate catered lunches on Wednesdays for faculty from other departments, and we staff ate and drank the leftovers the rest of the week. Cold cuts, cheeses, fruit, and lots of good wine. We would start our happy hour on Wednesday at four at our comfortable desks.

The dean of the school was an authority with an international reputation. When his secretary went on vacation I was asked to substitute because I could take shorthand. The dean would call me in and dictate a dozen or so one-sentence letters and sometimes one-word letters to his international colleagues. Having entered into the middle of these written conversations, the brilliance of his scholarship eluded me. In fact, sometimes I struggled to maintain the reverence he seemed to expect, biting my cheeks so my giggles would not leak out. To be fair, he was responsible for establishing a new academic discipline and had assembled a stellar faculty.

I climbed higher into the Berkeley hills when I was hired to work for a newly formed institute with a distinguished, Latin sounding name housed in a rental on Grizzly Peak. I had some misgivings when I noticed that the demarcation between the living quarters and the business office was only a hazy concept. From my desk in the living room, I could see into an unkempt kitchen and on to an unmade bed in the bedroom. One morning I arrived at the expected 8:30 time, but it was clear from their disheveled appearance that my boss, still in his boxers, and his girlfriend had barely gotten out of bed and were not ready to go to work. Greeting the late risers on another morning I noticed a small mirror and razor blade lying on the coffee table near my desk. When I realized what it was, I decided this was not the party for me, and I resigned. Hallucinogens were all right; I drew the line at cocaine. I was there one month.

I managed to stay afloat between jobs by taking advantage of unemployment insurance benefits seven times. I don't know who was more dishonest—the wasteful spending at UC Berkeley and cocaine parties funded by research grants or my own opportunistic use of unemployment benefits. These payments did afford me the way to continue my personal search through art and my own therapy. I took art classes at Laney College and learned to draw. I did an intensive therapy process with a guide, spending the better part of every day for three months in self-analysis. That is very hard work. After I finished that process, Bill, with whom I was living at the time, said he noticed such a positive change in me he wanted the same thing for himself.

I hit the bottom of the jobs barrel when I was offered to interview for an admin assist job for a company in Oakland that made body bags. This is not a business I had ever considered, and I didn't have to think twice before declining that interview. I wondered if there was an opening because the incumbent had need of their product. It reminded me of the unassuming woman I worked alongside for a half-day in a salmon cannery in college. When I tried to initiate a conversation to make the time go by, she had nothing to say. She had worked for over twenty years just stapling boxes. Somewhere along the way she had given up.

The body bag job scared me. A wakeup call. I was in danger of drifting farther and farther down the career ladder. Actually, I wasn't even on the ladder. It took me considerably longer than the newly appointed hurricane chief to recognize my own hurricane. But I finally let the storm hit. I let it sweep me up to do the hard work of training to be a therapist so I could have the job I wanted.

## DEATH AND DYING

As both a skeptic and a searcher, I attended a death and dying conference in Berkeley with Elisabeth Kubler-Ross.

The weekend was overwhelming.

Her co-presenter Raymond Moody, MD, spoke first of his research with people who had had a near-death experience and were willing to talk about it. Many were reluctant to speak of it for fear of being laughed at or even committed, since the phenomenon was greatly suspect at that time. Medical doctors, especially, denied or covered up near-death experiences they had witnessed. On stage, brave Dr. Moody and four of his brave subjects described the white light, the tunnel, the tug by someone or something pulling them back to life. We could buy his book *Life After Life*, stories of survivors.

Dr. Kubler-Ross admitted she had communicated with her mother after she died of a stroke. From the beyond, her Swiss-German mother was stern, scolding her physician-daughter for not knowing that anyone who had had a stroke would have a terrible headache and should be given aspirin. That seemed plausible. The aspirin part, I mean.

After a two-and-a-half-day immersion in dying, death, and return to life, it's not surprising that I would be emotionally stirred up. These are provocative topics.

Friday and Saturday evening I did not mention the conference to Bill Two. We had recently moved from the group house and the big fight between Bill

One and Bill Two. He apparently thought I was wasting my time. I needed to protect myself. But when I came home Sunday evening I decided to risk telling him some of what I had heard. He showed only mild interest.

As I recalled the weekend, I began to cry. The crying overtook me. I couldn't stop. It wasn't about Bill's lack of interest. It was my response to hearing, over and over, that there was life after life and there were many who were willing to attest to it. I cried for over an hour, tears of cathartic relief.

Eventually the storm subsided and I returned to everyday life. I did not know at the time experiences like this were preparation for graduate school.

I continued to look for every personal growth experience I could find. When I heard about a psychologist who was looking for subjects for her research into past lives, I signed up. Dr. Helen Wambach would hypnotize us and invite us to discover a former life.

We met at 7:00 in the evening in Walnut Creek. I was surprised at the size of the group, about thirty of us crowded into her small apartment. As she dimmed the lights she told us to lie down on the floor, close our eyes, and make ourselves comfortable. I was miffed by her indifference to our comfort. The floor was cold bare tile. She at least could have suggested we bring our own mats. This would be an ordeal.

She began our hypnotic induction in an unremarkable way, saying simply to relax, let our minds quiet, visualize an earlier time, and let a scene appear. We were told to notice in that scene what we were wearing on our feet, to conjure a meal and take note of our utensils, and to make a monetary transaction. She would later correlate the descriptions of footwear, eating utensils, and money with historical periods to see if they matched.

I felt grumpy on the hard floor and thought I wasn't hypnotized but decided to just let my mind wander. This was the scene that came to me: I was a French nobleman wearing black shoes with thick two-inch heels, pointed toe and a broad black bow. I was also wearing white tights; Louis XIV style of breeches of white, yellow and turquoise satin; a silk brocade jacket; and a white lace jabot. I was in the middle of a large mirrored ballroom at a country chateau. Too powerful to assassinate, I was being held prisoner near the village of Rely. (I have not been able to find any such village on a map of France.) I was dancing round and round in a clumsy dance. I was insane with advanced syphilis.

During my imagined meal, a bulky woman in coarse clothing came toward me across the vast ballroom floor carrying food. It was gray, watery gruel in a clumsy wooden bowl with a wooden spoon. The utensils looked like they had been hacked, not carved.

During the monetary transaction, I was the same aristocrat, but before my illness. It was a stormy night. I was in a horse-drawn carriage, hurtling through the slick streets of Paris. I could feel my heart pounding with the urgency and danger of my mission for the French king. I was clutching a drawstring bag heavy with gold coins. I didn't think to remove one from the red velvet bag to look at it, which might have been useful for Dr. Wambach's research.

The induction ended and we were instructed to open our eyes and slowly come back into the room. I estimated I had been under about half an hour. I was astonished to find out I had been in a deep trance for three hours. She published her book in 1978, *Life Before Life*, based on her research.

I had one other past life experience under *self*-hypnosis. I was first a child cave dweller, wearing a coarse fur garment, dead with her head bashed in. I was a malevolent queen of ancient Egypt with three-inch black fingernails who had murdered members of

168

her family. I was an apple-cheeked nun on her hands and knees scrubbing the stone floors of a medieval abbey, humming. I was the wife of an eighteenth century astronomer gazing thoughtfully up at the heavens. These I took to represent aspects of myself—the injured, the vengeful, the believing, the seeking. I'm fascinated by the economy of the unconscious mind, choosing such an apt symbol for early psychological wounds—a child with her head bashed in. Or the spiritual me as a young nun performing the simple ritual of scrubbing the floor. And what better image for an angry self—a murderous Ptolemaic queen? I'm uncertain about the mad syphilitic French nobleman. As a child, I wanted to be a princess—perhaps an unhealthy choice.

When I mentioned these experiences to a friend, he dismissed them as unconvincing and said the only way to prove a past life is if someone recalls a life in a culture and place no one has ever heard of. That way we would know they were not influenced by known history, media or other people. Of course, then there would be no way to authenticate it. For me, though, the importance of past lives is not whether we have actually lived them but what a past life experience can reveal about unrecognized aspects of ourselves.

I went kicking and screaming back to school for my master's in psychology, even though it was the only thing I was truly interested in. Aside from the one bad experience, I knew the profound value of psychotherapy. I couldn't admit to myself for a long time what I wanted, instead taking lower and lower level clerical jobs. My self-confidence sank right along with them. Finally, I wasn't hired for those anymore either. It seems I had to reach a dead end and close off all other options before I could face the immense project of becoming a licensed therapist. I knew there were more therapists per square inch in the Bay Area than anywhere else on the planet. I doubted I could ever make a living at it. I didn't think I could make the transition from patient to therapist. I felt it was presumptuous to think I could do the work my own therapists were able to do. While I had them on a pedestal, my self-confidence was at its lowest point.

Yet once I admitted that's what I really wanted, something grabbed me by the throat and wouldn't let go. It's like the story Annie Dillard told about a hunter who shoots an eagle. At its throat hangs the skeleton of a weasel which wouldn't let go when the eagle took off. It's her image for living the dedicated life. Deep inside I knew I could help people as I had been helped. Nothing else felt as valuable or important.

I started out with a prep course for the required GRE (Graduate Record Exam) and then took the exam. I scored in the ninety-seventh percentile in language and an embarrassingly low thirty-third percentile in math. That means that only three percent of college graduates in the U.S. scored better than I in language and sixty-six percent scored better in math. Uh-oh! With no aptitude for math, I enrolled in a course in statistics, a prerequisite. If I couldn't pass statistics, I might as well give up. Luckily, I found an instructor who taught the course without the need for algebra. To my surprise, this was the most enjoyable class I took in all of my graduate work. Stat was fun. I loved the instructor for making probability theory fascinating and for opening the door to graduate school. I got an A.

The thing that had me by the throat did not let go even though I had no car and planned to use public transportation to get to school. I was immediately challenged by a bus and a BART strike. It took half a day on "bus bridges" to go from Oakland, where I lived then, to Cal State Hayward where I was to meet with my advisor, Dr. E. She asked me what I wanted to take. I mentioned two courses and she snapped, "You can't take those!" I snapped back, "Why not?" She snapped again, tensions rising. Finally, I said, "I don't think I'll be able to work with you as my advisor." She: "Well, you'll lose your place in the program then."

Feeling sick, I found the administration office where I was told to start classes and select my own advisor when I found someone I liked. I chose Dr. M, who accepted me, reluctantly. As the semester progressed I learned that my original advisor was known to be unpredictable and arbitrary and was even feared by some faculty. My new advisor was concerned Dr. E might retaliate against him in some way for accepting me.

It was a good thing I did not continue with Dr. E. She intimidated me, and I don't do well when intimidated. I had applied to a state school because it was cheap, and I had no money. I told myself it was simply a necessary ticket to the next level of training. I found out later there was stiff competition for a place in the program. This was a close call. In truth, I was scared to death. The academic side of the program was secondary to the psychological. The instructors did need to weed out people who were not appropriate. I didn't know how they did that, and the ambiguity was terrible. This graduate program was a test not so much of academic ability but of personal strength under challenging scrutiny. I was neither strong nor confident. I had been painfully and slowly reclaiming my sense of self-worth lost in the twenty years between college and graduate school. I was afraid my instructors would discover that I was emotionally unstable and therefore unfit to be there. I *was* emotionally unstable. I was deep into my own therapy where one is asked to temporarily put aside defenses in order to delve deep and eventually replace ineffective defenses with healthy ones. In my vulnerable state, every instructor felt like a hanging judge. I was in a blizzard without a coat.

Dr. E taught one of the required core courses—sex therapy. My advisor informed me that Dr. E would bar me from her class, effectively making it impossible for me to complete the program. He suggested I do an independent study to fulfill the sex therapy requirement. Read a book, write a paper, and attend a workshop. I found a whopper of a workshop. The SAR (Sexual Attitude Restructuring) weekend at the Institute for Sex Research in San Francisco was designed by former Methodist ministers who had trained with Alfred Kinsey, a pioneer in human sexuality. Friday night through Sunday afternoon we lounged on red-carpeted risers and enormous pillows in a windowless, softly lighted, brothel-like amphitheater listening to presenters talk about sex among the handicapped, the paralyzed, gays and lesbians, the elderly, and everybody else.

Saturday evening was the climax, so to speak, of the weekend—the "Fuck-o-Rama." The founding Methodist ministers had traveled the world filming people having sex in sensuous settings—in the woods, on tropical beaches, at the mountains. They also had a library of Kinsey films and regular old porno films. These they projected simultaneously on all four walls, the ceiling, the floor, and us. There was nowhere to look without seeing people having sex with each other, people with animals, animals with animals, people in nuns' costumes, or failing to perform at all. The point was to help us be more comfortable with sex. Several of us went out for dinner afterwards. I accepted an invitation from another student to go to a nearby hotel to test how successful the weekend had been for us. I don't remember his name and I never saw him again. We rated the weekend a success. I was certainly having more fun than I ever would have had in Dr. E's class.

I borrowed $11,000 in student loans, at three, five and seven percent interest. My parents gave me a thousand dollars and I got a part-time job, so I used very little of the loan money. Instead, I put it into a savings account paying eleven percent interest, so I made money on the loans and paid them off soon after I finished school. Hmmm. Maybe I was on the right track after all. Goethe noticed the phenomenon that when one commits to a dream without hesitation, no turning back, forces mysteriously converge to support one's goal. He called it Providence. I can attest to that.

I gritted my teeth and stuck with it, the weasel always at my neck. From GRE to licensure it took me eight years—two years of school, five years of unpaid internships, and one year of preparation for licensure squeezed in and around part-time office work. When I opened the envelope containing my new license, I didn't whoop, I didn't call anyone, I didn't go shopping. Without thought or conscious intention, I went to the kitchen of my rented apartment and began digging out the rotten grout in the 1920s chicken-wire tile on the countertop. I dug and scraped for hours until I got all the black, gunky rottenness out. I went to the hardware store for new white grout. After all those years of abstract thinking, I wanted to get my hands dirty and do something gritty and muscular. The grout was just the thing.

Then I had to start a practice. Providence and the weasel stayed with me as I did more traveling along the way to a successful practice.

Psych internships were hard to find. My school did little or nothing to help graduates find them, and they were required for licensure and independent practice.

I did one of my five, unpaid psych internships at the Federal Correctional Institution (FCI) in Pleasanton. I don't recall how I heard about this one at the federal prison. I didn't even know there was a federal prison in the Bay Area. I wasn't particularly interested in working with that population, but the pressure was on to pile up as many hours as I could so I could start a practice and begin making a good living. After a brief, nonthreatening interview with a prison psychologist, I signed on for a nine-month internship. I would be accumulating a lot of hours and would even be paid a small stipend.

Because the inmates were not management problems (i.e., not violent) the officers (guards) were not armed except at the far perimeter of the chain link fence. The well-kept campus could pass for a suburban office complex with its parking lot, one-story buildings, and wide lawn. The double chain-link fence was barely noticeable. The inmates called it "Club Fed." FCI Pleasanton housed a variety of offenders. Patty Hearst had been an inmate there. Ronald McIntosh, convicted of murder, escaped during a prison transfer. One month later, he landed a stolen helicopter in the exercise yard and liberated his bank-robbing girlfriend, Samantha Lopez. Had the officers been armed, Ronald and Samantha could not have pulled this off. Even following that, the officers remained unarmed. A Catholic nun had been there earlier doing time for civil disobedience.

Unfortunately, there had been an "incident" at one of the other low security federal prisons in the country, so visitors and staff had to be escorted by an officer in and out of the facility and between buildings. This was tedious. I felt imprisoned myself. When I asked what the incident was, I got only an evasive response.

I was given the job of interviewing new arrivals to assess their mental state and tell them about the counseling services available to them. That way, I built up a small clientele with whom I met once a week. Although it was a coed prison, all my clients were men, probably because there were more men than women inmates.

I felt uneasy with only one of the inmates. He was a Hispanic L.A. gang member, convicted as an accomplice to murder. Full of sneering attitude, he tilted back in his chair, flashed his tattooed knuckles, smoothed his oiled hair, and told me I should be at home taking care of babies. I ignored his advice. He declined my services.

For our protection, our offices had windows on all sides so that patrolling guards could make sure we were safe when meeting alone with a prisoner, as well as track inmates. Forget privacy, even in a therapy session. There was nowhere for a prisoner to sit alone and read, unobserved. The only door without a window was the lavatory/shower, and even there the door had a four-inch gap at the bottom.

FCI Pleasanton housed federal prisoners, those convicted of federal crimes or who came under federal jurisdiction. These included Native Americans, drug smugglers, embezzlers, mail frauds. There was a considerable number of non-English-speaking Central American women who had been implicated in their husbands' drug deals. When one of the psychologists realized there were eight bank embezzlers in the prison, a therapy group was started just for them. They were usually from a lower middle-class background and happy to have a respectable job (obviously, not happy enough). The temptation was too much for a new bank teller. As the group members talked, it emerged they used the money not for themselves but to buy gifts for family members to show they had achieved middle class affluence. I was not asked to lead this group. I suspect it was considered a plum job, and it was given to one of the more senior interns.

My most regular client was a man who had stolen Social Security checks from mailboxes to finance his sex change operations. He had had genital reconstruction, and the next surgery would have been to have his Adam's apple shaved to a more feminine size. When I asked him about his motivation for changing his sex, he told me he thought it was easier to be a woman than a man in our culture. I silently disagreed with him but did agree with Stanford's gender reassignment unit that this was too flimsy a reason for them to accept him. He had had his surgery elsewhere, and I believe it was botched. Apparently, my client thought so, too. I got reports from the prison physician that he neglected his genital hygiene. He would get infections,    occasionally smelling bad.

I felt great empathy for him. In our case conferences with the psych staff, I learned that he had no friends in prison. I was the only person inside he had any relationship with. He was shunned by the other inmates. The prison doctor was obviously disgusted by him. The guards either avoided him or were verbally abusive. He was housed by himself since there were no facilities for inmates undergoing gender reassignment. His only visitor was a blind woman. I often wonder what became of him. He had been given a long sentence. Stealing Social Security checks out of mailboxes is considered a very serious crime.

Near the end of my internship I closed the curtains to my office for some privacy with my transgender client during our session. It so happened that a count was conducted while we were meeting. These were random and unannounced. When it was discovered that one person was missing, there was a complete lockdown of the prison where everyone had to report to his or her room. This shut down all operations (laundry, kitchen, shop, etc.), and wasn't lifted until our session was over and the missing person—my client—appeared. I didn't know about the lockdown until I opened the door. No one said anything to me about this infraction. I know it was a serious one, and I've always wondered why my supervisor didn't mention it. Perhaps he wanted to do the same, just to have a bit of privacy. My client must have enjoyed the privacy as well. He had to know I was breaking the rules by closing the curtains. In his silence, he was complicit. My internship was nearly over. I believe my rebellious self was tired of complying with the rigidity of the prison system.

Shortly before my internship ended, a new prisoner was brought in. The prison was abuzz with the arrival of "Torchy." Torchy was from the South, the wife of a much older country pastor. Torchy had discovered that an acquaintance had had sex with her husband. Torchy got even by staging a drunken orgy in the woods with the woman and a few friends. First, she got her rival drunk. Then she gave her gasoline to drink. Then she lit a match. "Torchy." The other inmates were afraid of her. I passed her in the hallway once. I felt a dark shiver. She had red hair. Her blue eyes were blank.

My last client had jumped bail for marijuana possession in New York many years earlier. He had fled to the Caribbean under an assumed identity and eventually became a captain of charter yachts. He looked the part—tall, tanned, handsome. This would have been fun if my internship were not ending. I missed out on vicarious trips through the Caribbean with a handsome yacht captain. During his years in hiding he would occasionally sneak home to visit his parents in Santa Barbara. He lived a glamourous leisurely life for twenty years, although he frequently had to change his identity to avoid discovery. He told me he turned himself in when he no longer knew who he was. He was awaiting a hearing. His future was uncertain. He was preparing himself for a long sentence.

I told myself I was fine with being at the prison. I felt privileged to access an institution closed to most. I met people I never would have met. I got to know the prison shrinks who warned me that all inmates would con me if they had a chance. That I should be very skeptical. It's true that most of my clients started out protesting their innocence. I simply ignored that and went to work with them on more important issues. For the most part I found the men I worked with sympathetic people.

When I walked out of the prison for the last time I was surprised how relieved I felt. I hadn't allowed myself to realize how tense I had been those nine months.

It's true that jailers are as imprisoned as their charges.

As a newly licensed therapist, I mulled over whether I should buy malpractice insurance. I sourly thought to myself that I had nothing, no assets to go after, only debt. I had an old junker of a car and I was a renter. So why spend the money? Caution won over self-pity, and I bought a policy.

Almost immediately I was sued for malpractice. I was stunned. A mistake, surely. This is what happened: I had contracted to provide short-term counseling for a company called Occupational Health Services (OHS). The manual given to me as a provider included a statement saying that when they referred a patient I should not ask that person to sign a release of information permitting me to discuss his/her situation with a case manager at OHS. OHS had that handled in their central office. Don't bother the client with needless paperwork.

WRONG!

My first client referred by OHS was a man who worked for the ATF—Bureau of Alcohol, Tobacco and Firearms. The case manager at OHS asked me to evaluate the man for depression and report back to him. He had been referred for counseling by his supervisor who thought the man was in emotional trouble. His colleagues had heard him threatening to ignore mandatory and precise procedures required to do his job. As a bomb demolition expert, he was essentially threatening suicide and homicide.

When I met with him he could hardly talk or hold his head up he was so weighted with depression. His long-time girlfriend and their son had moved to Arizona. Their relationship was in doubt. He felt abandoned. He mentioned he had been adopted, psychologically often considered as the big abandonment. He admitted he was suicidal. He had considered taking himself and his colleagues out with his ready access to means. He agreed to another appointment and he left.

I immediately called the case manager who then called the man's supervisor. There's a law called Tarasoff which allows therapists to break confidentiality when a person is thought to be of danger to himself or others. His case seemed straightforward. I was not privy to what happened next, but several months later I was sued for gross negligence, malpractice, breach of confidentiality, loss of income, and on and on. I had to sweat through a grueling deposition as the opposing attorney challenged my training and credentials. I was freshly licensed and inexperienced. I thought Tarasoff would protect me. It felt hugely unfair.

I longed to get away and put all this behind me. Luckily, I was packing to leave for a two-week trip to Spain.

I later found out the bomb expert had fled, prompting a five-state manhunt. Officials first went to his home but did not enter, suspecting it had been rigged with explosives. Eventually he returned to the Bay Area and filed his worrisome lawsuit. The case was settled out of court. My insurance paid $10,000 on my behalf. OHS had to pay $20,000. The whole thing was deemed a "nuisance" suit, but I am now listed in the National Practitioner Data Bank. It's the place to go to find out if a professional has done bad or illegal things. Surprisingly, it has never interfered with my career. No insurance company has ever turned me down as a provider. Essentially, I was found innocent of any wrongdoing.

Now I ask every patient to sign a release of information if only to submit a bill to their insurance company. I learned my lesson.

I practiced for over thirty years. Some patients I saw only a few times—one to five sessions. I barely remember them. Others are more memorable.

One of my first patients in private practice was a woman in deep distress because she needed to tell someone about her history. She had never told her husband and felt like a fraud. She had married very well and lived in a wealthy, exclusive city where she felt she did not fit in. She had not told any of her friends believing they had never suffered as she had suffered.

Her mother could not care for her and sent her to a convent at about the age of six. She never heard from her family again. She was worked like a slave until, as a teen, she escaped the abusive environment of the convent. She made her way to New York where she slept in doorways, found menial work in restaurants, got an education, and eventually was admitted to an elite Eastern college. I was amazed at her grit, courage, and skills at survival. I also wondered about her relationship with her husband, her reticence to reveal herself. She did not stay long in therapy. If I had been more experienced, I could have helped her. I hope she found the courage to speak.

For a brief time, I saw patients in my home. I was a provider for an insurance company covering Chevron employees. They were usually high-functioning people. One evening I met with an employee for a first-time appointment and asked what brought him in. He went straight to the point: "I sometimes have a strong desire to hurt people." Without missing a beat, I asked, "Are you having that feeling now?" He said no. I was pleased that I came up with the exact question I needed to ask at that moment. I felt calm, not at all threatened by my patient, who seemed tense and embarrassed by his revelation. I said I needed to refer him to someone who was an expert in his problem, that I was not the best person to treat him. This was not true. I could have continued seeing him, but I did not feel it was wise to see him in my own home. I was essentially isolated with my patient, even though neighbors in my condo were next door.

I was referred a young man for depression and loneliness. He worked for a defense contractor, lived with his parents, and worked a 3 a.m. shift by choice, effectively preventing him from engaging in any social or dating activities. He was resistant to seeing how self-defeating his schedule was. He also told me he collected rifles which he stored under his bed. When semiautomatic rifles were to become unavailable for purchase online, his mother had offered him the use of her credit card to purchase eight more to add to this collection. He told me he would sit on the edge of his bed drinking whiskey out of the bottle while fondling one of his guns, putting the muzzle in his mouth.

I was angry with this guy for his guns and whiskey nights. I was angry with his clueless mother. I wanted to shout at both of them. Instead, I steered away from the gun conversation and back to the reason he came to see me in the first place—his depression and social isolation. He discontinued therapy after a few sessions. It was easier for him to flirt with personal destruction than to face his social awkwardness and try flirting with a woman instead.

I saw Camille for many years. She had been sexually abused by both her father and her brother. Psychologically devastated, she was heavily medicated. I watched her deteriorate and thought she should be referred elsewhere. She would not hear of it, but instead became even more tightly attached to me. She was in love. She wanted us to go away together. She would do almost anything to have more of me. At times I felt she wanted to climb inside me, even though she could not look at me. I knew from her husband she spent her days between sessions lying in bed, almost catatonic. Eventually he refused to drive her the three hours to our bimonthly appointments, and we said goodbye. Our work had grown toxic for my patient. I was relieved he insisted on discontinuing, both for myself and for her. I knew she would be redirected by her psychiatrists to more productive group psychotherapy.

Eunice also became attached to me in an unhealthy way. Much of her story was about being a serious fan of a famous person, traveling around the country to attend every performance and appearance. She had graduated to stalking. In her manic determination to be close to this person, she traveled to Europe, found the person's home, gained access over double walls and through security systems, and broke in and stole intimate apparel and letters. One day it occurred to me that Eunice had probably stalked me. I was a sitting duck for her. I asked her if she had. She admitted it, made no excuse. I told her that if she ever did it again her therapy would be discontinued immediately. Since Eunice was not even close to her goal in therapy to convince me we should be friends forever, I believe she discontinued stalking me.

It was a tearful day for Eunice when I closed my practice.

Ruth was memorable for a different reason. Not only was she not attached to me, she told me she disliked me, that she did not care what happened to me, did not care whether I had a happy life or not, would never think about me once we ended therapy. I was at a loss, for a moment. I did wonder where she learned to be so baldly disagreeable. Then I asked her why she kept coming if she thought so little of me and really didn't like me. Grumpily, she admitted I made her think. Okay, if good enough for her, good enough for me.

It was spring quarter at the end of my two-year master's program in psychology when I decided to take advantage of a free service at the school and went to the career counseling center. The tests showed my interest and aptitude were strongest in interior design, not psychology. I was dismayed. When I mentioned this to one of my instructors he said, "Think of psychology as interior design of the mind." He said exactly the right thing to reassure me, and I continued with psychology. He was probably a very good clinician.

My passion for interiors began as a child. All my life I have succumbed intermittently to its glamor. As a child I loved making a "room" under the dining room table. Mother would hang a large blanket over the top to enclose the space beneath. My sisters and I would play under there for hours. But the best room was one I had all to myself upstairs under the eaves of the finished attic. I arranged four wooden orange crates to make a platform which I enclosed with a light blue gauzy cloth hung from a clothes rod. I laid a pad on the crates and covered it with pink satin left over from the harem girl costume Mother had made for Halloween—blue gauzy pantaloons, pink satin girdle and vest. After school, I would put on my harem costume and crawl into my gauzy retreat. I believe it was rehearsal for my dream of growing up to be a princess, a common childhood aspiration. I didn't know that harem girls were concubines, not princesses.

The most fun I ever had furnishing a space was in San Francisco in the early 1970s when my roommate Gail and I rented an old house on upper Market. My bedroom was the dining room where walls, floors, built-in buffet, and boxed-beam ceiling were all the original, darkly stained wood. To lighten it up I painted the floor high-gloss taxi cab yellow. I didn't bother to prep the floor. After the paint dried I noticed a small bump. I had painted right over a smashed raisin.

I sewed together four yellow and brown Indian bedspreads from Cost Plus and enclosed the ceiling. I added a daybed, an antique trunk and a large white flokati rug. It was a yummy retreat.

When we were moving out the owner came to inspect for any damage we might be liable for. I arranged not to be there, leaving my roommate to face the owner. I can only imagine his reaction on seeing the yellow floor. Apparently, he said not a word.

Much later when I was licensed and starting private practice, I started with not one office but two- only ten miles apart. I reasoned that I could maintain a larger practice by serving two different communities. But I suspect no small part of that was the itch to shop for just the right artwork, area rugs, just the right lighting, just the right seating, twice.

A few years later I heard about newly remodeled offices on College Avenue in Oakland. As I toured the complex I could hardly breathe looking at the hand-tinted plaster walls, an entire wall of banked windows above wood cabinets, the custom window shades, the sage green carpet, the double doors for extra soundproofing, the subtle lighting. I chose the largest one and found a partner to share the exorbitant rent.

I suspect one of the more compelling reasons to move to Portland in 2007 was to upgrade a townhouse I owned there. What fun shopping for wooden slat shades for seventeen windows, cork flooring and carpet, an oversized black kitchen sink with just the right fixtures. And the *pièce de résistance*, a disappearing screen for the front door, custom-colored to match the exterior trim, with a magnetic latch. My only regret is that the place was in Portland, not Oakland.

However, three years later I was to indulge myself again when I moved back to my condo in Oakland. I wasted no time replacing old vinyl floors in the kitchen and bathroom with custom ceramic tile. I installed handsome slab granite countertops in the kitchen and bath, and sleek new sinks and fixtures. New wall-to-wall carpet, new draw draperies. And the ultimate—a self-lowering toilet seat.

It's been several years since I finished this project, and I'm feeling awfully antsy.

# JIM

I have skipped celebrating many July Fourth weekends since my relationship with Jim ended in the early sixties. I met him when I first moved to San Francisco. He had a beautiful apartment in Pacific Heights, an Austin Healy sports car, a VW Bug, a sailboat, and a cabin at Tahoe. His mother was social secretary for Lurline Matson Roth, for whom the Hawaii-bound *Lurline* luxury liner was named. Lurline's home was called Filoli, a grand country estate on sixteen acres in Woodside. (In 1975 she donated it to the National Trust for Historic Preservation. Today Filoli is a popular tourist destination.)

Mrs. Roth had season tickets to the San Francisco Opera. When she did not use her tickets, she gave them to Jim's mother who would occasionally give them to Jim who would invite me. Fourth row center orchestra. I was leading the glamorous Bay Area life. What was not to love? Well, him.

Even so, we had a standing Saturday night dinner date in Tiburon where we always had martinis first and then ordered a bottle of Louis Martini cabernet sauvignon and filet mignon. We never called the wine just "cab," as now.

Jim liked to cook, and some Saturdays he invited one or two other couples for dinner at his apartment. Guests were asked to arrive at eight. I would go to Jim's about seven to help him get ready. Trouble was, Jim was barely out of his bathrobe until about nine. It took me a while to catch on. His friends knew better

190

than to arrive on time. I too began arriving later and later. When I complained about the lateness, he would just smile. I suspected he very much enjoyed annoying people, such as me. It worked.

We spent major holiday weekends at his cabin in Tahoe—Memorial Day, July Fourth and Labor Day. I still associate these major weekends with Jim's Lake Tahoe cabin. The cabin was a plain, uninsulated wood structure that he and his father had built. Nothing fancy; just the necessities of running water, electricity, and a wood-burning stove. He would invite about ten of his friends for a nonstop drinking weekend, one bloody Mary after another in the morning and martinis and a steak dinner in the evening. No one was interested in any active sports like hiking or swimming.

That was the zenith of my glamorous San Francisco social life, ending with a hangover. The sixties came after, but they were more gritty than glamorous.

## JACK

I met Jack when I had moved back to Oregon in 2007 and was attending a university class reunion. I had known who he was in college but he probably didn't know who I was. He and a fraternity brother would walk from sorority to sorority at dinner hour and perform short comedy routines known as "flying skits" to promote campus events. We always looked forward to Jack and Gordy. They were two campus darlings, Jack as easygoing as a sloth and Gordy movie star handsome.

At the reunion Jack stayed close by my side during the winery tour and later at the university president's reception. He told me his wife of many years was very ill, dying of cancer, but she had urged him to go. The next evening at the cocktail hour prior to the banquet he suggested we sit together at dinner. Jack was easy to be with. I loved the attention. I couldn't help wonder about his obvious enjoyment, what with his wife dying and all.

I left for home having given Jack my phone number and email. Two months later Jack called and said his wife had died. He said he was in his van with his dog. He was going fishing and just wanted to talk for a bit. When he called again after another two months he suggested we get together. It had been only four months since his wife had died. It seemed way too soon.

I started dating him anyway and heard his stories. First, I told him mine, about San Francisco in the sixties and the characteristic adventures of that era.

He could not relate to them at all. I think I shocked him. But probably not as much as he shocked me with his revelations about his marriage. In his forty-year marriage he had had two consecutive twelve-year-long affairs. He would tell his wife he was going fishing. I asked him if he ever brought fish home. No-o-o. He added that he didn't think his wife knew. I choked. He said the worst thing would be if his children found out. He was less concerned about the judgment of his wife than of his children.

Now, nobody didn't like Jack. He was a thoroughly lovable guy, and I was getting attached, letting my fantasies grow. He had a wonderful house which needed some warming up. I'm good at that. He had a very nice sleek dog, important, since I don't like many dogs. I even thought I could tolerate living in cold, rainy Portland if we were together. I found myself attaching significance to our coincidences. We were born the same day, same month, same year. We were fated. I thought maybe I had met my soul mate. I even found myself blurting out, "I love you, Jack," over dinner one evening, surprising myself. I had never done that before. I ignored the warnings about his philandering ways.

When I first stayed over at Jack's house I thought we should sleep in the guest bedroom out of deference to his dead wife. We did a couple of times; then he moved us, apparently unbothered, into their bedroom. We were much more comfortable in a queen than a double. I wondered about the propriety of sleeping in their bed. I looked at her clothes, still hanging in the closet. I was trying to get a sense of who she was. I went through drawers in the bathroom looking at her cosmetics and jewelry. When I read a review of Barbara Brooker's book, *Should I Sleep in his Dead Wife's Bed?* I laughed. She had nailed my dilemma. Not sure what I'll do the next time I date a widower. I think I'll avoid the problem and go to my own bed.

In spite of our identical birthdays, I don't think we would have been a match. We spent a few days at his beach house. I learned he really was a sloth. He took two naps a day, one after breakfast and one after lunch. I would be out exploring, energetically walking the village and hiking the beach. He would walk the beach with me after his afternoon nap, but when we came to a steep sand bank I had to pull him up. He didn't have the strength to do it by himself. I like to travel, but he couldn't imagine enduring a long flight.

I moved back to California. We made plans for Jack to visit me in the summer. Jack rarely used email, but one day he emailed me to let me know he would not be coming. He had connected with a former girlfriend and had fallen deeply in love and was moving in with her. I was shocked and hurt. All I could do was crawl into bed and rock myself while I let sink in what I already knew at the beach when we had little to talk about; what I already knew when I wanted a picture of us standing close together with his arm around my waist and he moved away just a fraction; what I already knew when he was evasive about coming down to see me; what I already knew when he was not there to say goodbye when I left for California. I hurt anyway.

It didn't take me long to put the back-story together. I think he had started seeing his new girlfriend even before we went to the beach. When I realized his deception, I was angry enough to get over him pretty quickly.

Jack calls me on our shared birthday and we talk briefly. He still lives with his girlfriend. When he calls, I ask him if he is out fishing.

## Online Dating for Fun and Self-Improvement

More recently, meeting strangers through online dating has been a rich source of tips for self-improvement. On our second date, Chuck looked at me at a romantic candle-lit dinner and told me, disapprovingly, that I had no eyebrows. What an effective way to break the mood. No friend had ever mentioned it. When I got home I appraised my eyebrows in the mirror and saw that he was right. It's not true that I don't have any eyebrows, it's just that they're so light they don't show. So I began to draw them on. I now have those lovely arches I've always coveted in others.

Chuck did not endear himself to me and we had only one or two more dates. One evening we were walking arm-in-arm down Sutter Street when a stranger said, "Your daughter sure is good looking." Chuck harrumphed and I had to stifle my urge to laugh. The guy obviously wanted to rile him. We are the same age but he looks a lot older than I. It must have been my new, youthful eyebrows.

Another online acquaintance, Greg, quietly told me to wear paler lipstick. And he was right, too. Do these guys read fashion magazines? I don't, but then I started noticing the current less-color-is-more trend. If a suggestion is good, I'll take it.

Matt said he wondered about my intelligence quotient (IQ) when I told him about panicking and buying a new car in one day when my old car died and learned it would cost too much to repair. He told me he only wanted to date smart women with a master's or doctorate. I did wonder what had happened to my usual way of thoroughly researching a major purchase, but when my car died my thoroughness died with it. I noticed that Matt's empathy quotient (EQ) for my dilemma was at the low end of the scale, although I didn't mention it. I satisfied my naughty need to get even when, in a romantic interlude, I murmured that he could get his droopy eyelids fixed and that Medicare would pay for it if he could demonstrate they impede his vision. He said nothing. A second time I flunked his IQ requirement when I told him no, I had not written any professional papers and that I was writing my memoirs which is a lot more fun. His response was, "No one will ever read them!" This comment did not impel me to abandon my memoir-writing but it did suggest that I abandon the relationship.

I'd rather do something much more fun than drink coffee to launch a potential relationship, like watch the slackliners and jugglers at Lake Merritt or see what's happening in Union Square. But that would mean investing time in someone I might have little interest in spending more than an hour with, if that.

As was the case with Robert. He seemed like a good prospect when I read his profile: accomplished artist (he exhibited his paintings), an art teacher, loved the outdoors, nice looking. We agreed to meet halfway in Novato in Marin County at a Starbucks. He was there first. I walked to his table. He didn't stand. I sat down. He already had his coffee.

Eventually he asked, "Are you going to order something?" "Yes." It took me a moment to regroup. My coffee dates had always offered to buy. Since I was buying I decided I could have anything I wanted. I found something new on the menu and ordered a matcha latte, a powdered green tea frothed in milk with a bit of sweetener. It's bright grassy green and even tastes grassy. It's delicious and fresh.

We left Starbucks to explore Novato, and I asked him how online dating was working for him. He momentarily became real and told me he had had sixty coffee dates. I wondered if he might not be interested in anything longer than a coffee date. Rehashing the afternoon, I calculated that sixty coffee dates times $3.50 per latte comes to $210. That's a lot of money he would have spent on women he had no interest in seeing again. No wonder he didn't buy my drink. It wasn't only his frugality that discouraged my interest. He was deeply immersed in an offshoot of EST and I could not understand much of what he was saying since they assign special meanings to ordinary words. We didn't speak the same language.

Next time I met a date for lunch. Unfortunately, lunch takes longer than coffee. He didn't fit my modest criteria, but the novelty of cutting the pizza with a pair of scissors saved the day, and this time he paid.

With enough dates and enough suggestions for my improvement, I expect one day I'll be perfect. Until then I'm having fun with my memoirs, whether anyone reads them or not. And as long as I continue online dating, I'll have a steady supply of anecdotes to write about.

Online dating seems a circuitous way of discovering new food and beverage offerings. I can find those myself. Next time I try online dating, I'll plunge right in with what I'd like to do and suggest a trip to whale watch. Does he have a taste for adventure? Is he as awed by nature and wildlife as I am? How does he interact with strangers? How does he behave when he's seasick? On second thought, maybe a trip to check out Union Square would be a better start.

Some online meetings can be frightening, if not dangerous. I met Warren through a personals ad for supper on a spring evening at a sidewalk café on College Avenue. It was romantic and cozy under warming lamps and canvas awning. He was tall, slender, handsome, educated, attentive, and funny. When he told me, with an odd smile, that he was a rage-aholic, I should have excused myself then and there. Instead, I smiled a reassuring smile back. I thought, I'm a psychotherapist, I can handle that.

He told me his father had retired as a colonel in the Air Force and that he himself was a West Point graduate. That impressed me. But he did not seem "military." That puzzled me. His story unfolded. After graduation from West Point he had refused orders to be sent to Viet Nam. I don't know the consequences of that, but they were severe. He wouldn't talk about it. I can only imagine what his career military father might have said or done. Warren's right eyelid sometimes drooped. I suspect it was from a blow. He told me that in high school he had been sent to a military academy in Oregon, far from his Florida family. Military academies often are for forcing boys to become what their fathers could not force them to be. Reform school. I continued to ignore warning inklings.

For our next date, I suggested a picnic on the hills overlooking the ocean at Steep Ravine on Highway 1. I know how to woo a guy, and I know a good picnic spot. I wanted to show him one of my favorite places, a campground which gently tugs you into another dimension as you descend toward the ocean, compelling you to abandon care and let the magic of sun, surf and solitude carry you away.

I prepared my most seductive menu: potato salad with tiny pieces of pickled herring for an indescribable salty/savory flavor, chilled Sauvignon blanc, sweet French baguettes, creamy bleu Castillo, big strawberries, chocolate squares with lavender and sea salt. All intended to soothe a rageaholic. He was impressed and we continued to date.

I can't remember how things started to go bad. Without warning he erupted in anger at something I said. I have no idea what it was. Completely baffled and surprised at the strength of his anger, I asked to be taken home. I said goodnight without further plans. He called the next day. I agreed to see him. After several more such incidents I decided to end it. I said goodbye. All my training did not equip me to handle the extreme irrational hostility I was seeing. When I got home my phone was ringing. I didn't answer it but after several hours of ignoring the ringing, unplugging the phone, plugging it back in, more ringing, I answered because I needed to get to sleep. He pleaded, begged. I could feel myself pulled down into a vortex of emotional turbulence, endings, apologies, pleadings and promises.

I became ill one night with a Meniere's attack. For a number of months before meeting Warren I had been ill with Meniere's disease, characterized by nausea and severe vertigo. I had lost some of my hearing. I did not expect the attack that night. With prior attacks I had had warning symptoms. Warren got up with me and helped me to the bathroom where I retched and retched. He held my head, so gently, mopped my mouth and forehead, gave me water to rinse my mouth. Not a bit of revulsion. Besides my mother, I had never experienced such tenderness. I was confused by his caring. He told me he had wanted to be doctor. What had gone so terribly wrong that he had trained as a warrior instead of a healer?

About two a.m. my phone rang. I had left the volume on. He got up to answer it. In my groggy state I wondered about his answering my phone. I could hear a brief conversation. The next morning he told me it was his girlfriend of many years who had found my number. He had told me his relationship with her had ended before we met.

The next time he blew up at me I told him to stop the car immediately and let me out. Fortunately, this was only a few blocks from home. I made good on my vow that this was the end. He must have thought so too; this time he did not harass me with phone calls.

Later I asked him to talk with me one more time about what had happened. I needed closure and I needed to know the status of his relationship with the woman who had called at two in the morning. He was willing to meet me at my place one afternoon. My questions were too much for him. Again, the explosion. He ranted and raved, calling me a fucking whore among other epithets, and left, slamming the door so hard I'm sure it rattled the twenty-seven other units in my building.

I had a lot of responsibility for the catastrophe. Warren had warned me on our first date. I ignored his warning thinking he was exaggerating. If anyone ever again tells me he is a rageaholic, I'll believe him and run the other way.

THERE THERE
(Vignettes of Here and Now)

I had lived in the Bay Area for forty-five years. Until I left, I didn't realize how deep my roots were. I didn't marry. I didn't raise a family here. I wasn't sure this was truly home.

With great uncertainty, I decided to leave. I was seventy and thought I might like to retire. "Decide" is too tidy a word for the long, messy process I went through. The $130-an-hour therapist I hoped would help me feel better about moving was too good a professional to express an opinion. I knew I was unconvinced; otherwise, I wouldn't be in her office. I knew my voice lacked enthusiasm, so I redoubled my efforts to persuade her, earnestly listing all the good reasons to make the move. Then I would make an equivalent case for all the good reasons to stay. When I finally gave up the struggle for clarity, I knew that moving wasn't such a hot idea but soothed myself with the idea of returning in two years.

I closed a large psychotherapy practice, terminating all my clients, a lengthy and often painful process. I closed three offices and sold or gave away several roomfuls of furniture. I spent weekends for three months packing and stacking 125 boxes to the ceiling of my small living room. I easily could have been mistaken for a psychotic hoarder.

There were good financial reasons for moving. I had been renting out a townhouse in Portland purchased three years earlier with a small inheritance from my mother. I had claimed it as a business on my tax return, and when I sold it I would have to pay big capital gains taxes. If I lived in it for two years I calculated I could save about $35,000 in taxes. My fragile decision was shaken when a friend, unconcerned about expressing *her* opinion, said, "I'd never make such a drastic change for $35,000," implying it was hardly enough money for tearing up one's life. However, I came to like thinking about my project as drastic. It made me feel better. It *was* drastic.

The other good financial reason to move was that I would rent my Oakland place while I was living in Portland. After two years I would sell Portland and pay off my Oakland mortgage and have money left over. I would be set for life financially. I could live with ease, travel more. All the pain and labor of moving would be worth it. Then came the housing collapse of 2008, blowing my calculations sideways. I would still be okay financially, just not as robustly so.

I'm going to come out of the closet and admit where the idea to move originated. A psychic. I don't know how many people would admit to having consulted a psychic, let alone acted on the advice. (I suspect this is one of the last two crowded closets. The other closet is atheism.)

I was paying the psychic good money for her time, so I mentioned my Portland dilemma. She jumped on the idea, saying my "soul travelers" in the Bay Area had been exhausted. I didn't ask what soul travelers were, but I gathered I needed new ones who were not as tired as mine.

The reasons for moving were personal, too. For years I had mulled over returning to Portland where my family lives. I had been missing out on all the family gatherings—birthdays, Fourth of July parties, kids' activities. I thought I would put the question to bed by finding out if I liked living near my family. I imagined once-a-month family suppers. Or volunteering to shop for the great paper towel and toilet paper bargains at Costco for each household. They would be so grateful for my efforts. I thought my sister and I might become better friends and hike and go to play readings together. It was an entire year before she invited me to the play readings. We never did have extended family dinners. Nor was anyone interested in economizing on toilet paper. They pretty much continued their lives as always. Soon, old family tensions resurfaced as if I had not been away for nearly half a century. I felt left out—one of the family dramas I needed to escape when I moved to the Bay Area.

I underestimated how difficult it would be to make friends. My old college acquaintances had all the friends they needed, most having lived in Portland all their lives. Immodestly, I thought I would be bringing them a breath of fresh air, what with my Bay Area sophistication and world travels. No one noticed. I underestimated what a challenge it would be to learn a new freeway system, especially with twelve bridges over the city's bisecting Willamette River, each bridge leading to a discrete, completely unfamiliar neighborhood. The only time I drove over those bridges was by mistake. I did not know how much colder six hundred miles north could be. I didn't realize that summer heat would last day *and night* without an ocean nearby. And when I did go to the ocean a hundred miles away in mid-August to cool off, I needed a thick sweater and windbreaker against the wind, cold and fog.

If I had new soul travelers there, they didn't introduce themselves.

All told, the Bay Area spoiled me for living anywhere else. I realize I am seldom bothered by what others find so annoying here—traffic, other drivers, the high cost of just about everything. I'm grateful for the energy, grateful for the number of people walking, shopping, sitting in coffee shops. I need a large population. When I returned to Oakland after three years in the North, I thought I had arrived at a resort—weather so perfect, the sky so bright, few heavy black clouds to block the sun. The real differences, though, are not chamber of commerce items but my memories. In Portland I felt empty, poor in spirit for want of memories of the place.

The Bay Area is home because of the years spent here, where my thousands of experiences have been laid down in the strata of memory, like fossils telling the story of my life. My next adventures I expect will produce a rich trove of fossils for the newest layer of my geologic life, my Oakland Grand Canyon.

I love the crush of the seven million people who live in the entire Bay Area. In Portland people peer into your face to see if they know you as you pass them. At first I liked it but later came to mutter silently, "Of course you don't know me. I'm completely new here." Because Portland is small in comparison, chances are you might know the person you are passing. Not in the Bay Area. That's just fine with me. I cherish my anonymity. I'm not a small town girl.

The legendary tolerance of the Bay Area has a flip side: friendships can be instant, and then over. Superficial. It's much easier to be tolerant if you don't have to get too close. Even though friendships can be fleeting, before they flee it is wonderful to hear a friend's story. Acquaintances have told me about their estrangement from family; financial difficulties; mastectomies; abortions; divorces; their addicted, murdered or incarcerated relatives. They have told me about the book they're writing, their travel destination, their restaurant finds. I got the impression I would need to know my Portland acquaintances for a long while before they would divulge any personal stories to me.

I think I know why. Portland is a smaller city, and the circles of acquaintance are smaller. It's harder to maintain one's privacy, free of scrutiny or gossip. So people are careful about who they let in. I can speak more freely here because what I divulge to my friend won't circulate back to my grandmother, my aunt, or my mother. There's a good chance our circles of friends don't even overlap. You might say Portland is a vertical town—many have lived there for several generations. I prefer a city where people have migrated horizontally across the country to settle here, without the pressure of extended family.

So tell me your stories, your secrets. They're safe with me.

## THE SINGER, THE WIFE BEATER, THE NAZI, AND ME

I love the diversity of Oakland. I'm not talking so much here about ethnic diversity as about diversity of the peculiar and exotic, which I have in abundance right in my own building.

I live in a condo. The tenant above me was a singer with a big voice. She would sing at top volume from her deck. The street was her concert hall; the acoustics were good and so was her singing. Pop and jazz. Clearly a pro. I enjoyed her performances except for a long, explosive cackle after each song. Her laugh was as loud as her singing, resonating for blocks, though not a laugh of pleasure. She was laughing at something no one else could see or hear, an unsettling sound suggesting something unhinged. I never met her and one day the music was over. She had moved away and new tenants moved in.

They were loud too. I could hear thuds and thumps and angry yelling. I could hear her hitting the floor. The unmistakable sounds of domestic violence. Call the police? Knock on their door? I delayed, amazed at myself for my confused inaction, especially because of my training as a psychotherapist. The terrible sounds continued. One day I went upstairs to give them a piece of misdelivered mail. I wanted to see who these people were. The man opened his door just a crack, looking at me with such menace I shrank back as I handed him the envelope. When I heard him knocking her around I could imagine him attacking me. I feared that if I called the police he would retaliate. After I heard the sliding glass door crack as one of them crashed into it, I knew I needed to do something before one of them was killed. I talked to the two women who lived in the unit next to them. They listened for the man to leave, brought her to their unit, and found a shelter for her. She was from Eastern Europe, barely spoke English, and unaware such help was available. I called the owner of the unit who got rid of the man by immediately putting the unit up for sale.

These are the major characters. One of the lesser players is the newest owner above me. She is quiet as a pin except when I hear something dropped on the floor three or four times, like a large piece of furniture or perhaps a heavy barbell. I am stumped. She does seem to have trouble keeping her grip on objects, especially in the kitchen where I can expect her to drop a pan or two at dinnertime. This is not a problem for me, since most weeks she is away traveling on business. When I do hear a pan hitting the floor, the predictability is comforting.

Then there was the Sikh who wore a bright pink turban any baby girl would coo herself silly for. He told me he would be running his twenty-fifth marathon that Sunday. He could not have astounded me more had he told me he could walk through walls. Maybe he could.

Bernhard rounds out our diverse community. Bernhard had been trained as a Hitler Youth in Germany and had been drafted into the army at the age of nineteen near the end of World War Two. He had been sent to the Russian front, and when the

Germans surrendered he was taken to a Russian prison camp. He told me no one cared about defeated German soldiers in a remote prison camp, and knew he would probably die there. He thought his only chance was to starve himself, hoping the Russians would send him to a rehabilitation camp he had heard about. The Russians had uses for strong, healthy German prisoners. He indeed was sent to an R&R camp from which he escaped, walking from Russia through Europe and eventually reaching the U.S. Much later in his life he moved into my building, with his Hitler Youth training and its anti-Semitism intact. I know this because Bernhard would not ride in the elevator with David, a Jew from New York.

## Dem Bones

The *toe bone* is connected to the foot bone. The *foot bone* is connected to *three hip bones*. The hip bones are connected to *four rib bones*. The rib bones are connected to the *shoulder bone*. The shoulder bone is connected to the *wrist bone*. The wrist bone is connected to the *hand bone*. Now hear the word of the Lord.

I've broken enough bones to qualify as a Hollywood stuntman. Twelve in all.

The first, in 1965, was on a three-day backpacking trip over Labor Day weekend near Mammoth Mountain ski resort on the east side of the Sierras—a long way from San Francisco. This was a new sport for me. I was invited by the good-looking guy with that musical Irish lilt who lived across from me on Green Street. I borrowed a pack and other equipment and set out—eight of us in all. On the way out I slipped on the smooth granite and broke my arm. No one warned me that wearing canvas sneakers with smooth rubber soles and carrying a heavy backpack was a bad idea.

One of our group was a doctor, but when I looked to him for help he backed away spluttering that he "hadn't had bones for several years." He didn't do a thing to help me. Just then two angels in the form of wiry, seasoned backpackers appeared and jumped right in. They splinted my arm with a red farmer's bandana, gave me painkillers, and trotted off. We redistributed my pack and hiked to our cars, three hours away.

Pain is an odd phenomenon. Knowing we had to keep moving, I could keep the pain at bay, but in the car, as we were nearing help, I began to lose control. When we arrived at the pharmacy adjacent to the hospital, I could stand it no longer and sank to the floor wailing, "I need help **NOW**."

Fortunately, the doctor there had "had bones," lots of them, since it was a ski resort. In a lovely haze of pain killers I said goodbye to my backpacking buddies, had my arm set, and was admitted to the hospital where I stayed for two days, but only on the condition that I could have an evening cocktail. I was humored and was served vodka and orange juice before dinner. The doctor joined me. I suspect there was no vodka in it since I was on painkillers, but I was flattered that a busy doctor had time to socialize.

It was time to go home and the doctor said he would fly me to Reno where he was going for a flying lesson. I could get a plane from there back to San Francisco. A flying lesson? I hoped he was an experienced pilot. The Bridgeport Hospital docs served all of Mono County, remote and sparse, by plane. His was a tiny, two-seater. In spite of being terrified, I count it as a highlight in my life. I suspect terror is one ingredient of a highlight.

After arriving home in San Francisco, as I told my roommates my story, I burst into tears. It's called crying at a happy ending. And, happily, I pampered myself with six weeks of visits to the salon for shampoos, manicures and massages.

My arm was cast at a right angle, like a long, white glove. When I was invited to the opening night of the

San Francisco Opera (Leontyne Price, "La Forza del Destino," September 1965), I wore a long white glove on my left arm and made a sling for my right arm out of a pink ribbon to match my satin, sequins and feather boa. Our picture was taken as we arrived but we didn't make the fashion pages of the *Chronicle* the next day. My classy escort Randy, one of the Green Street Gang living across the street, had made after-opera reservations for us at the Top of the Mark for *crepes Suzette* and champagne. We were young, gorgeous, and every bit up to the sparkling, gala evening.

The other eleven bones? A cracked rib skiing at Squaw Valley. Five in a cycling accident—three in my pelvis, my shoulder and my rib, as well as a hole in my lung—when I veered into deep gravel. Ten days in a hospital in Canada and three months on crutches. My foot, tripping on uneven pavement in front of my condo on the way to the market. My left hand, the dominant one, tripping on stairs and lunging for a metal railing while exploring Emeryville. Two ribs when a dog knocked me down. One big toe when I tripped on stairs.

I suppose I have more bones I could break if I were to take up, say, racquetball, skateboarding, or basketball. But I am forced to concede that I am not much of a jock and so will confine myself to walking and hiking. I have purchased a pair of nifty hiking poles to outwit the treachery hidden in such gentle sports, unless I trip on my own poles.

## Free Nuts

I buy two-pound bags of salt and pepper pistachios at Costco and dump them into an air-tight container when I get home. Sometimes pistachios fall out of their shells on their own. I call them free nuts. Free because there's no tedious work of having to split open the shells. An instant munch. I'm surprised at the burst of pleasure I get when I find one. A treasure hunt right in my own kitchen. Every time I open the container I shake it and hope to find a free nut, even though I've probably found all the escapees.

I feel like a chimpanzee as I hunt for free nuts. He pops a flea into his mouth, I pop a nut. Both crunchy. The pleasure of the hunt. This ancient, hominid ritual probably releases serotonin.

Ever since my pleasing discovery I have looked around for other free nuts and have found many. When I hit every green light weaving my way past double-parkers on Piedmont Avenue. When my cyclamen continues to bloom untended by me. When I am dealt a good hand in bridge, just sitting at the table waiting for the cards to be delivered. When a friend emails me a truly funny story. When a hummingbird stops by for lunch.

Others might call these moments blessings. I do too. But it's more fun calling them free nuts.

The Woodman. I loved a man in Oregon who didn't believe in spending money. He certainly had enough but insisted his former wife economize by buying only skim powdered milk for the family. His twenty-five-year-old car smelled of rotten plastic. His second wife couldn't stand the smell and bought him a new one. Before he had his house built he dug up scores of seedling fir trees to avoid cutting them down, and then replanted them around the new house. His house was constructed almost entirely of side-by-side two-by-fours. How he reconciled this lavish use of solid wood with his save-the-fir-trees campaign he could not say. He was a man of few words. He was an avid woodcutter and would speed out with his chainsaw to cut up any downed trees he had heard about. He had stacked firewood around his property, labyrinth-like. He had twenty-three whole cords of wood spaced around his lot. I wondered about the habitat he had provided for rats and spiders and other varmints. As with most people with a streak of eccentricity, he did not care what people thought about his peculiarities.

The Gambler. My brother-in-law's brother was a professional gambler. He was also a graduate of Reed College and a newspaper editor. But his heart was in poker-playing, and he left the paper to pursue his passion. He too didn't care what people thought about him. Each weekday morning he would kiss his wife goodbye and say that he was "going to work." He would leave the house as if dressed for an office job and head to the card room where he "worked" all day. I think he did all right, but his wife prudently kept her job at the bank, just in case.

The Toenail Man. I met a tall, lanky man at a party. He invited me to drop by sometime, so a girlfriend and I went to visit him one Saturday afternoon. He and his roommate were renting a house just off Fifty-first and Broadway in Oakland. Their sunny, bright living room was unfurnished except for the glass cases lining all four walls in which they kept their large collection of snakes. I remember how echoey the room was, without any furniture to absorb sound. We sat on the floor drinking tea as I nervously eyed the snakes. Then I noticed the roommate's toenails. I forgot the snakes. When you let your toenails grow long, they can curve upward at quite an angle. His did. He said he was working toward a Guinness record. They were ugly—thick, yellow, and gnarled. He had trouble walking and couldn't wear shoes, so he rarely left the house. It was the male version of foot-binding. His roommate did all the shopping, including the mice for the snakes. I didn't stay long and was not inclined to visit again.

Acid Man. The young guy who lived in the rear garden apartment in my building on Fillmore and Pacific in San Francisco told me he took LSD every day. His apartment was always dark, the better to enhance the effect I suppose. In my experience there is a marked diminishing return with LSD. Mainly I felt nothing more than a slight buzzing in my head after three or four times. I accepted when he invited me to trip with him one Friday evening. Nothing much happened. Except with my cat. At some point in the evening I went into the bathroom where my annoyed cat had left a deposit in the corner on the tile floor. If anything is more nauseating than cat shit, I don't know what it is. But I needed to use the bathroom and was in no mood to clean it up, so I told myself I couldn't smell anything. To test my powers of self-suggestion, and with no little apprehension, I took several deep, slow breaths as I sat on the toilet. I smelled nothing but clean, fresh air. It worked. That was fun.

The Camino Walker. I met a woman in Portland on a hike. We talked about our vacations. She said she and her husband were going for a stay on the private island they owned off Vancouver, BC. After that they were going to their Florida fly-in. Fly-in? They owned a house in a fly-in complex where you land your own plane and taxi into your own hanger and walk down the hall to your own living room. Can't you just imagine! Her telling was low-key, matter-of-fact. She was not trying to impress. This was just her life. Then she told me about her experience walking the thousand-year-old pilgrimage route of Camino de Santiago in Spain. It is said that St. James's ashes were carried along that same route to be buried in Spain. Many people today retrace the route which they try to complete in a month—490 miles in thirty days, over sixteen miles every day. Many walk only sections of it, but she walked the entire route. A week into the walk she was hurting. A lot. She desperately wanted to finish, so she began to pray, as hard as she could. She prayed all night. The next day she walked thirty-five miles and the next day after that and the next day after that. For three days she walked thirty-five miles a day. People later told her they could not see her feet touch the ground. Those who walk the Camino say they are transformed in many subtle ways. She knew something extraordinary had happened to her, and I believed her, a pilgrim, simple and humble as any other, but with a private island and a Florida fly-in.

I cannot see myself clearly, but a young boy at the Portland airport was sure he could. I was having a quick bowl of chicken soup at the Flying Elephant deli before returning home when a young couple with a boy about five came to sit on the red banquettes next to me. They seated themselves and told him to scoot in next to them. He pulled back and whined, audibly, "I don't want to sit next to that old lady!" We all laughed, the parents very embarrassed. I still chuckle about this and then think what an ill-behaved child. He'll have some troubles ahead. Maybe I'll find a way to inflict them on him.

I'm genuinely startled when I board a crowded BART train and someone jumps up to offer me a seat. Sometimes I accept to humor them. Maybe it's the only considerate thing they've done all day. Other times I'm grateful to have a seat.

I don't see myself as elderly at all. The problem is that the body ages but the idea of the self does not, so there's a big disconnect between how others see me and how I see myself. Strangers offer me a seat on the train; meanwhile, I'm preparing for a safari in Tanzania.

Some of my contemporaries have moved into senior residences and others are on the cusp of doing so. I try to imagine it for myself. I look at the glossy brochures showing well-dressed, attractive people socializing on the patio, wine glasses in hand, all slender and young looking. But that headline "senior" is there, though printed in invisible letters. To me it has an ominous feel, like "Work Sets You Free" over the entrance to Auschwitz. Senior residence brochures are coy, seductive and false. You go there and you will die there. I think growing older is something like having a younger self tugging on the right hand and the older self tugging on the left hand. Neither will let go, in continuous struggle. Moving into a senior residence feels like letting the left hand win.

I have a few ideas about how to better align the inner and the outer. First, hair color. Ditch the gray. And then possibly another nip and tuck or two around the neck, so that when I next meet a five-year-old kid he might bring me a present, like a PEZ out of his backpack, instead of getting away with being a brat.

## DR. FISH

Until I went to Japan I didn't know how smooth my feet could be. And clean, really clean, after a fish pedicure.

You know how unpleasant your feet can be after walking around all day in sweaty shoes on dirty concrete. Well, you can expect smooth, nice-smelling feet if you have an aquarium stocked with one-inch, flesh-eating fish.

We arrived at an open-air mall selling Japanese handicrafts and saw a sign, "Dr. Fish." I didn't know who he was, but what drew me were the benches. We had done a lot of walking that morning and were ready to sit and rest. Then we saw the tank full of tiny fish.

We paid our ten dollars, sat down on the floor and slowly lowered our feet into the sunken pool. Scores of miniature cannibals raced to our feet and legs to nibble greedily at the dead skin. Between toes, under toenails. Some seemed to prefer my legs rather than my feet. The Japanese have some unusual preferences in the taste and texture of their food. Perhaps their fish do too.

I resisted a strong urge to pull my feet out and stayed until I could relax and enjoy the odd experience. The fish never seemed sated and fed as long as we kept our feet in the water. When you stop to think about it, it's pretty creepy to allow fish to feed off your feet. If you *don't* think about it, it's that indescribably delicious feeling of being lightly tickled.

I had a client once who was unhappy because her husband wouldn't tickle her back. If he would, it would make her feel loved  and cared for. I wish I could have told her to build a tank and stock it with tiny, fishy cannibals.

I am once more pushing myself to learn something difficult, playing duplicate bridge where players move from table to table playing the same hand to see who can wring the most out of it. It's a harrowing three hours for me, and I consider it a good evening when I can control my anxiety enough not to do something really stupid, like failing to follow suit or forgetting what suit we're playing in. I'm not even close to the place where I try for the best score.

I am well-acquainted with anxiety. It's my double, and appears whenever I try something new, taunting me, like Joel Gray's scary white face in *Cabaret*. It greets me when I wake on Tuesday morning and sits with me all day until it's time to leave for bridge that evening. It went to college and graduate school with me; it went through my licensing exam with me. It went skiing with me and accompanied me to my piano lessons as a kid. It has led a full life. As the first child, my father heaped lavish praise on me at the dinner table when I said something he considered clever. "Carol knows everything," he would say. I loved his fatherly pride, but he had no idea the burden he was placing on me. I might have been a quick study in the third or fourth grade, but I've slowed down considerably since then. His unwitting pressure on me as a child, which is now my own pressure, causes me lots of anxiety when I'm struggling to learn a new convention in bridge, and it sinks in as slowly as a feather in sludge.

I continue pushing myself because I still must want my father's praise. He's been gone since 1984. Some parts of ourselves never grow up.

## NEW YEAR'S RESOLUTIONS

I never make New Year's resolutions, and my decision that morning probably wasn't one either, since January was almost gone. I decided to make my bed soon after arising. I always liked seeing my bed flat and smooth, the decorative pillows doing their decorating, but not enough to pick them up off the floor and place them artfully puffed just so to hide my hard-working night pillows. That morning, as I surveyed the arranged bed with satisfaction, I realized I felt more ready for the day, suggesting I could expect a similar pleasing order to my day ahead. A made-up bed now is not only for company but for me too. I used to bother only for visitors or guests. I think of Emily Dickinson's poem, "Wild Nights" when I see a tousled bed, although I think Emily had something else in mind besides not making up one's bed.

Now, why all this about the bed? The rest of my home is tidy. Once a house painter I called to give me a bid looked around and, in amazement, asked if I were Japanese, which I am obviously not. There is nothing out of place.

After my mother began to expect more of us in adolescence, I rebelled by not making my bed. When my father was home I couldn't get away with it. When he was away my mother would usually do it for me. Her exasperation was no match for my stubbornness. When I moved out on my own I continued not making my bed. A messy bed is such a feeble way to express adolescent defiance.

I was joyfully confirmed in my not-doing when I came across a thousand-page book on every conceivable aspect of housekeeping (*Home Comforts, The Art and Science of Keeping House,* by Cheryl Mendelson). It had never occurred to me that maintaining a house could require so many words. Intrigued, I looked up bed-making and, to my delight, I learned that the best scientific practice of bed management is to fold back the blankets and sheets and let them air out until midday while you attend to other household demands, rendering your bed a much less hospitable environment for the dust mites which customarily inhabit it, and virtually guaranteeing a peaceful night's sleep. In my book that was permission not to make my bed at all.

If my January decision holds, an ordered bed first thing in the morning may cancel Cheryl Mendelson's guarantees of a healthful night's sleep, but I'll have the illusion of controlling my day ahead. And it is beyond time to let go of my adolescent rebellion.

I attended a Thanksgiving potluck where friend Jean had brought an indescribably delicious mashed potatoes dish. It was the melted butter pooled on top, of course, but it was the mixture of finely chopped, sautéed scallions, leeks, garlic, and onions that sent it over the top. She gave me a copy of the recipe from *Sunset*, a reliable source of good recipes.

As I made a copy to send to my niece for her files, my fantasy for Christmas dinner this year unfolded: Niece will call and say, "Good recipe! This dish can be your contribution for Christmas dinner this year." I'll quietly say, "No, I'm not cooking anything." If she protests, as I know she will, I'll remind her that no one in the family, almost without fail, has liked my contributions. One Christmas it was the matanzas, an elaborate Argentine dish of flank steak stuffed with baby carrots, watercress, green olives and hard boiled eggs and braised in a full bottle of Malbec. They said it was dry and a disappointing substitute for the traditional prime rib. No, they did not like the moist, deep chocolaty, chewy brownies with blood orange-infused olive oil I brought to the beach last summer. They preferred Mother's recipe— dry and crumbly. And, no thank you to the glorious chocolate cheesecake I serve with whipped cream and fresh raspberries. Niece does not like cheesecake so no one gets any. (She's the hostess.) And there was nothing not to like about the delicate smoked salmon I made by layering it with lapsang souchong tea. It was just a little tea-colored. But they didn't like it.

I admit I have been harboring food resentments for a few years. I just hope my niece follows the script so I can lure her into my ambush and make my big announcement. I'd rather let everyone else cook for me anyhow.

When I decided to return to school for my teaching credential I took only one interesting class, Introduction to Modern English. The rest were forgettable.

We read Ernst Cassirer, who theorized that the development of language began with a response to, say, a fall, and out came "ugh" or "uh." Little did the creature know what he or she had started.

I've always been interested in word derivations. I also sometimes have a vacant mind into which wanders a lot of nonsense. One day the word "slut" wandered in. Other sisters of the "uh" sound followed—smut, glut, scut. The "uh" sound seems to be right for conveying the meaning of these words. You need to push your diaphragm up with a bit of effort to make the sound.

Slut is a fun word. It's from "slattern," meaning slovenly, sexually promiscuous. You can also use it with chocolate. I am a slut for chocolate, or . . . fill in the blank. Or you can take the SLUT in Seattle—the South Lake Union Trolley.

Then there's smut. Sexually vulgar; something sexual in a dirty, pornographic way. I like *schmutzen* from Late Middle English. The extra syllables of *schmutzen* are especially pleasurable in the mouth and let you linger in the sense of vulgarity for just a moment longer. Another handy variant is the Swedish *snusk* meaning contemptible person. Smut is also a fungus and something to do with bad, soft coal. But irrelevant here. We're looking for juicy, with

230

connotations of . . . well, how about lewdness— lascivious, driven by lust or wantonness?

Then there's scut, as in scutwork; drudgery. One submission to Wikipedia was "menial, unfinished tasks, such as those left to medical students." This med student clearly was not happy with having to clean up and dispose of bits of flesh left after an anatomy class.

There are many more "uh" words, like putz, klutz and schmutz. Watch for the appropriate moment to use one of these *bon mots*.

These thoughts came together over one Memorial Day weekend, when I assigned myself all the scutwork I had avoided for many months. Since I'm usually a slut for cleanliness, I could no longer stand the slovenly look of my windows and cleaned off the smutty grit. Boy, did I look like a snusk then, but I had earned the reward of a glut (from gluttony) of cold, white wine.

## SERENGETI MIND

I became my animal self in the Serengeti. Eating, sleeping, washing, hunting. Animal rhythm. Silent. Only the necessary alert: "There's a giraffe, there's an elephant." The peace of few words. Immobile in the midday heat, with the wildebeest and zebra.

In our safari Jeep we moved slowly next to the lions as they loped among the vehicles. They were indifferent to us, while these creatures made us go mad capturing images of them as fast as we could. We looked silly in the face of their nonchalance.

If I were to take home one animal friend from the Serengeti it would be the wildebeest. Endearing in its mismatched parts, it is said to be assembled from leftovers: the face of a grasshopper, beard of a goat, horns of a buffalo, rear end of a hyena, legs of a cow, tail of a horse.

My animal self thinks about food as much as does the gazelle or the wart hog. Always, following safety. Hyenas are born with teeth. When mother is away hunting, the stronger babies eat the weaker ones. Only the strong survive. I watched vultures and marabou storks picking at a zebra carcass. The vulture's long, sinuous neck allowed it to reach deep inside the carcass between the skeleton and the hide to get at what was left after the lions had finished. Hyenas were waiting their turn to crack the bones. Marrow is moisture. All creatures were waiting for rain, as were we. The rains are uncertain in the Serengeti, as they are at home in Oakland. Maybe I'll have to suck marrow bones.

Deep in the Serengeti we slept in tents. On animal time—in bed by dark and up before dawn. I slept hard, drugged senseless by the daytime heat. Some of us heard the nightly snuffling of Cape buffalo, grazing near the camp where they were safer from lions. The buffalo have a reputation for being dangerous without provocation. I was too exhausted to care whether or not we were safe from buffalo or lions.

Just outside our tent was a canvas basin on a collapsible stand where we could wash and brush our teeth. In the dark, cool early morning a camp worker would fill it with very hot water. I can't remember ever feeling so grateful for something so simple. In fact, water is not simple. Water is heavy when one must carry it for miles. Just one gallon weighs almost eight and a half pounds. For much of the world, water does not come from a tap; it comes only with hard labor. Back at home, I stared in amazement as it flowed from the spout. I was overcome with gratitude. Shall we someday carry water on our backs? Be careful with water. One day we may no longer be better off than most of humanity.

At home, I was surprised by my need for the silence of the savannah. I wanted no radio, no TV. In church, I could not listen to the pastor's sermon; it was distracting after the silence of the savannah. Conversation detoured me from an inner peace as vast as the Serengeti. I was sleeping half my days. I think I could have slept even more. Not as long as the lion who is awake only three or four hours a day, but my meals do not take as much speed and cunning to capture.

The Serengeti was harsh and hot. With the beasts, I struggled for survival trying to keep my blood from boiling over. At home in a milder place I lost touch with my animal self. It crawled deep into its lair to a place I don't know. I'll need it again someday—when thinking is useless, when my animal self tells me to just be still and watch.

I had not planned on a personal pilgrimage when I traveled recently to Portugal, Spain, and France on a cruise. One of the shore excursions was a walk of a portion of the Camino de Santiago or, simply, The Camino or The Way. This was one of three most important pilgrimage routes in the Middle Ages. The most important destination was Rome. Second was the Camino in Spain and the third was Mont Saint-Michel off the coast of Brittany in France.

Life was hard and harsh in the Middle Ages. The church taught that humans were born with original sin and needed salvation through the church. They were poor, cold, and hungry. Little education, almost nonexistent health care, crude sanitation and lighting. The only hope for most was the afterlife, with its beauty, warmth, and comfort. Earnest pleas for forgiveness on a long, dangerous, and arduous pilgrimage might get one there.

I regretted not being able to walk the Camino because I was in a walking cast with a broken toe. (I had been quite disorderly at a weekend at Sea Ranch. After too much imbibing, in the dark I forgot about the three stairs to the living room and pitched forward.) I thought of the woman who walked thirty-five miles per day for three days, inspired by her fervent praying to complete the walk. But I was determined not to miss Mont Saint-Michel, no matter what it took, foot-wise. As the magnificent abbey loomed ahead of us with its impossibly tall spire, its gold statue of the archangel Michael brandishing his even higher sword, I knew I was living a lifelong dream. When I was in college, every dorm room had a poster of mystical Mont Saint-Michael.

So I began the long, steep climb up the stone stairs to the topmost courtyard of the abbey. Three hundred steps in all the guide told us. There were landings along the way, to be sure. There were overlooks where we stopped to catch our breath. But the guide was not exaggerating the number of steps. I counted them. Thank God there were handrails.

We arrived at the courtyard with views of the Atlantic. Each block of stone on which we stood bore a mark: C, 8, or 1. It was the signature of the stone mason who was paid by the block. Mr. 8 was especially ambitious. I hope he was paid well. The stone blocks were huge.

Eventually we were led down into a crypt. This is when I realized I was on a pilgrimage after all, not a vacation tour. I prayed not for forgiveness of my sins but for sure footing as I descended the narrow, spiraling staircase, barely able to see in the dim light. I struggled to plant firmly my bulky walking cast at the narrow end of the triangular step. As in pilgrimages of old, the descent was a test of personal strength and courage, of intense and focused concentration. As in pilgrimages of old, I begged for protection from danger. I had put myself in a situation from which I could not turn back. I hung on to the handrail for dear life. When I stepped off the last stone step several people congratulated me, marveling at my courage. Or possibly my foolishness.

My first bad trip was to Mexico. Not bad, really. More like interesting bad. I met a man, went out a few times, and when he asked if I would like to accompany him to Manzanillo, Mexico, at Thanksgiving for a family reunion at their timeshare, I said yes. I barely knew him but I thought we would remain platonic, with several of his children and their spouses there as "chaperones." It wasn't an especially generous offer, since I had to pay my own airfare. The condo was spacious and everyone had a bedroom. When I was suffocating in the hot weather, I'd escape to the lazy river canal which encircled the pool. It had a strong current so no effort was required.

In casual conversation I mentioned I was a member of the Sierra Club. You should have heard the contempt: "That commie, left-wing, bunch of radicals! Obstructing honorable chemical, mining, lumber, and oil companies!" I almost dropped my strawberry daiquiri. I was among foreigners. My hosts, I mean. Better be careful. Then I began hearing the term *gold-digger*. Did they mean me? I didn't want any of their gold, I just wanted a pleasant trip to Mexico. They worked very hard to conceal their wealth. I had seen how my host lived, wearing slovenly clothes, driving a beat-up car full of junk, sailing a rundown sailboat. He had the disreputable look down pat. His daughter's luggage was held together with duct tape. When I commented that it had seen a few miles, she said, "Look closely. This is new." She told me she

237

had left it unlocked and unguarded in the Mexico City bus station and no one had touched it.

Back home we dated a few more times and then he told me I dressed like a schoolmarm and that he realized he liked trashy women. I wonder if he has found a trashy, wealthy woman so he can stop worrying about gold-diggers.

China was a bad trip, too. I dated Boyd a few times when out of nowhere he asked me if I was interested in going to China. China? It wasn't on my list. Several of his friends were going. I thought a ready-made group of traveling companions was something I should not turn down. I again would be paying my own way.

We were to share a room, so I bought demure pajamas that looked like street clothes. Since I didn't have a brother, it was fun to imagine Boyd as my brother. I don't know what he thought of me, but it soon became apparent he was pretty skittish around me. We confirmed with the trip organizers that our room would always have two beds. Of course, the first hotel we checked into had a double bed. Two single beds soon arrived and the staff tried to stuff them into the small room already tightly occupied by a double bed. What were they going to do, stack the singles on top of the double? They seemed flummoxed by this dilemma, murmuring among themselves, until I began forcefully gesturing to them how to make the switch. Boyd stood aside, mute.

Beds were finally swapped, and I suggested we go down to the bar for a nightcap. This was the last enjoyable social moment I had with him on a three-week trip. Boyd didn't sit by me on the bus or at the breakfast table. He didn't talk to me. I think he was afraid the others would think we were a couple, or that I would. I saw him only once after we returned home. It took me a while to realize he had used me to avoid paying extra for a single room. That was a few years ago, and I have yet to look at my China photos.

SAYULITA SUN

Sayulita is a dusty but "discovered" beach town about an hour north of Puerto Vallarta. Americans and Canadians have built expensive casas in the hills at the north end of town. Outdoor showers and tubs, lots of stone tile, banana leaf roofs over twelve-foot ceilings, infinity pools, views of the Bay of Banderas. I recently spent a week there with eight members of my family in one of these elegant homes. We could swim in the infinity pool and see the beach at the same time. I much preferred the clean, calm swimming in the pool to the ocean. The strong surf can be dangerous. I don't like getting sticky with sun screen, which doesn't do much to prevent sun damage but does an excellent job if you like being coated with sand. Everyone in the family professes to love the beach, so I helped assemble beach equipment— enough stuff to set up housekeeping for several days. All morning we gathered and loaded towels, chairs, shade umbrellas, boogie boards and beer coolers into the golf carts we had rented to transport ourselves up and down the hill just to roast ourselves stupid in the hot sun for a couple of hours. To cool off I would sit in the surf and accept the penalty of a bathing suit full of coarse sand. I would make my way up the hill waddling like a toddler with a diaper full of poop.

Sun and Mexico always remind me of college friend Jean. She has spent winters for the past twenty plus years tanning at the beach in Puerto Vallarta. When one spends that much time in the tropical sun, tanning produces skin like a fine Italian handbag, but

240

with wrinkles. She is a dark shade of teak. Tanning—whether tanning a cowhide with chemicals or tanning your own skin for years in the hot sun—produces the same result: leather.

One summer Saturday, boyfriend Richard and I were in Sonoma, and I suggested we find Jean. She lives there the other half of the year and works part-time arranging flower and vegetable displays for an organic farm. We found the farm in the Valley of the Moon. I introduced Jean to Richard among her artfully displayed tomatoes, carrots and eggplants. Without missing a beat, Richard snorted, turned around and stalked out. I made it a point not to hurry out to the car where he was waiting. I wasn't going to indulge that kind of rude display. Richard couldn't find the words to express his disgust at seeing Jean, and his revulsion was palpable. Yes, Jean's appearance is startling. She has crystal blue eyes which flash like sapphires from her leathery, wrinkled face. She shouts when she talks, when she isn't whispering. She can be sharply emphatic. She is puzzled that her little granddaughter does not come to her readily. I think the child is afraid of Jean, with her piercing blue eyes, loud voice and dark skin. Sometimes *I'm* afraid of her.

Back in Sayulita, I did my best to protect my skin from any more sun damage than I already have. If I had started a steady tanning process when Jean did, maybe I would be brown instead of dotted with little white sun-damage scars. And if we hadn't had two teenaged boys with us, I'll bet the other adults wouldn't be so keen to spend a sweltering, sticky afternoon at the beach either.

## An Experienced Traveler

I did not realize how experienced a traveler I had become until I went to Mexico with my sisters. They have not traveled much. Patti questioned the price of the simplest transaction—whether coffee, orange juice, or a bottle of water. Converting dollars to pesos by dividing eleven into one-hundred and then multiplying the result by, say, nine is not easy when there are others waiting in line behind you and the coins are not familiar. She would fumble and try to calculate what her drink cost in dollars. My philosophy is if I want a bottle of water I'll pay what is asked and trust I'll get the correct change. I don't care what it costs in pesos. Patti always needed to know.

While Patti is a nervous traveler, Sharon is a timid traveler. She stuck close to me when we explored the shops near our hotel. I was proud of her, though, when, on her own, she bargained for and bought a piece of artwork at a shop where the staff spoke little English.

I sensed the tension rising at the Puerto Vallarta airport when I was directed to one kiosk to check in and the sisters and my nephew were directed to another. Patti gets flustered and has difficulty focusing. Sharon won't wear her glasses so she can't read the computer screen. And nephew Christopher doesn't use a computer at all. In the press of people trying to check in, an agent saw them floundering and came to their rescue. What they don't know is that airports are superb at handling and directing crowds of people, many of whom are as anxious as my sisters. Usually there is only one way to go, whether through security or to your gate or to claim your baggage. Except at the Athens airport. I haven't been there for ten years, but I'm inclined to think their airport is still as much a mess as their economy. I would not suggest Greece for our next family adventure. Maybe Bozeman.

## Latin—Dead or Alive?

I'm attempting to memorize the "Lacrymosa" of Mozart's *Requiem* as our choir director has suggested. There are only eleven words but I cannot relate them to English. To me it's gibberish. So far, I'm only working on the words. The music that goes with them will take another major effort but one which will make more sense. I can read music. I'm hoping that the magnificence of Mozart's music will bring Latin to life once again. I won't know that until I can put the words and music together.

I can understand some Spanish. And French and even Italian. But Latin. Never have words seemed so devoid of nuance or color. They seem as jumbled as the fallen marble columns of the ancient world. Does Latin have any exuberant verbs? Does it have any perfect adjectives or adverbs to blow you out of your seat with the power of their message?

Oh, there are some useful words and phrases we still use, like *vice versa*, *carpe diem*, *ad nauseum*, *status quo*, and *in vino veritas*.

Maybe Latin deserved to die. Did it die of neglect, wan and pale for lack of exercise? Who was the last Latin speaker? I wonder if people one day decided it was prudent to speak the language of the conquering Goths, Vandals and Visigoths. Or perhaps Latin left in a hush, like the gradual fading of voices as lights dim in a theater.

## The Jazz Singer

The Chapel of the Chimes at the end of Piedmont Avenue in Oakland next to Mountain View Cemetery is, to my way of thinking, the most beautiful building in the entire Bay Area. A maze of small, light-filled, marble-tiled rooms, the walls are lined with niches for cinerary urns in the shape of books. That's Julia Morgan's fine touch—one's life as a book. The chapel was enlarged and renovated in the late 1920s based on her architectural plans and incorporating her favorite Moorish and Gothic styles. The staircase was originally designed for Hearst Castle, her largest project. Around every corner of the chapel is a fountain, a sculpture, or a garden or ornate stonework. There is no finer resting place.

Technically it's a columbarium. As a wordsmith I needed to know the derivation of that word. It's from the Latin *columba*, meaning dove and originally referred to compartmentalized housing for doves and pigeons called a dovecote. Thus, the dead, gentle as doves, with stories to tell.

A partial list of those in books or chalices at Chapel of the Chimes: Al Davis, Oakland Raiders' owner; John Lee Hooker, musician; Joe Knowland, owner of the Oakland Tribune and U.S. Congressman; and Friend Richardson, California governor. I had never heard of him but included him because of his descriptive name. Almost as good as Goodluck Jonathan, former president of Nigeria.

The chapel occasionally sponsors jazz concerts and I went to one on a recent Sunday afternoon. A female jazz singer accompanied by piano and bass. The bass player was Marcus Shelby, a well-known Oakland musician and one of the most handsome men around. Uncomfortable bench seating but wonderful acoustics. I learned a lot about jazz singing that day, hearing Kellye Gray use her voice the way another musician would experiment with an instrument. At times she sounded like a baby delighting in playing with her toes. Whoops, cheeps, chortles, twitters, moans, yelps, whispers. She was having so much fun playing with her voice I thought she would break out laughing, but she was a highly-controlled professional who could take you to the edge of vocal madness and back. When I got what she was doing, I just grinned.

It's a sweet way to spend a Sunday afternoon, in synch with the loopy, goofy music of an edgy jazz singer among the resting, quiet dead. I hoped that the physics of sound might have tuned the ashes in nearby urns, settling them into deeper repose. Thank you, Chapel of the Chimes, from all of us not-yet-ashes.

## BELLY DANCING

Belly dancing is back. I noticed a new studio on College Avenue. I wonder if their classes are as big as mine was in the early 1970s. About forty of us met in a gym in Sausalito once a week. I wondered how our teacher came to teach belly dancing. A man, small and wiry, from Turkey. Even without hips or a belly he could demonstrate the moves well. We were his harem. We would form a large circle and dance barefoot round and round. Our teacher watched us from the center of the circle.

In my early thirties, I had some doubts about being able to belly dance. As a kid I had been okay with tap dancing, but it was less than a month before ballet and I parted company. Tap-dancing classes lasted for two months, but when word got around about the creepy teacher, who today would be known as a pedophile, my mother quickly pulled my sisters and me out of the class. In high school I could learn the cheer leading dance steps; belly dancing was different.

The best part of belly dancing was the costume. The metallic clinking of the coin belt and ankle bracelets, gauzy pink pantaloons slung low on the hips, scanty satin top to expose the fat bellies, flat bellies, jiggly bellies. And the exotic finger cymbals. We clanged and jangled our way in the big circle, trying to tilt back and thrust the hip out, just so. No matter how I tried, I always felt stiff and jerky. Most of the other women were not born to belly dance either.

But one was. The teacher would occasionally ask Jeanie to demonstrate a move or a step. She was as supple and fluid as an eel, dancing effortlessly, weightless. She could roll and flutter her flat, tanned belly from sternum to naval as easily as waving her hand. Her dancing was beautiful. We sighed at her fluidity, knowing that would never be us. It was like watching Suzanne Farrell or Baryshnikov.

I continued with belly dancing for about six months and finally had to admit I didn't have the kind of lower back that could tolerate all that unnatural tilting. I would miss the music, the exotic costumes, and the mystery of it. But most of all I would miss seeing Jeanie dance. I wonder what happened to her.

Belly dancing is a wonderful way to entertain one's spouse. Boyfriend Bill Two and I once spent an evening with friends at their home. The wife was an accomplished potter whose pieces were of museum quality. She was also a lovely belly dancer. She danced for us in the living room in full costume. Her husband told us she regularly danced for him. I can't think of a more exotic, erotic, Saturday evening at home.

When my parents visited me in San Francisco, I wanted them to have experiences they would not have had at home, so I took them to watch belly dancing. We arrived early at the club in North Beach. We were the only patrons there. The dancer headed straight for my father and moved in close. He tried to move away from her, almost tipping backward in his chair, an undisguised look of disgust on his face. I didn't know the extent of my father's prudish reserve until that evening. He must have also wondered about me and my belly dancing, but he did not say, nor did he have any comment about the dancer. His face, though, said it all.

# THE GUITAR

Several months ago a short piece in the Oakland *Tribune*'s business section caught my eye. A Japanese guitar maker, a Mr. Yairi, had died. Yairi guitars have been made by several generations of the Yairi family. Their best guitars were said to be favored by Paul McCartney.

I have a Yairi which I bought in the 1960s with the help of my guitar teacher. I think I paid $125 for it, which was some money at that time. I'm sure it is not McCartney quality but I wanted to have it checked out and evaluated. Secretly, of course, I hoped it was one of Yairi's best.

I called a luthier in Kensington whom I had also read about in the *Tribune*. He makes fine guitars and repairs both professional and student instruments. That fact especially caught my eye. I knew mine was a student guitar. Just a few years prior I had taken it to a guitar shop in Berkeley. The guy who looked at it sniffed condescendingly and said, in effect, it was just a low average student guitar worth a couple of hundred, if that.

I decided to seek a second opinion.

Before I went to see the luthier, I replaced the strings. I had not played the guitar for perhaps twenty years and strings can go dead. It took me hours of unwinding and winding to get the old off and the new on. Actually, the new ones were old too. They had been resting in their envelopes in my guitar case since I last played. But I decided to put them on anyway and went to see the luthier.

My experience with him was much better than in the Berkeley guitar shop. He looked into the interior of my instrument with a periscope to examine the bracing; he peered at the length of the neck to detect warping; he tuned it and played a few chords. To my ears it sounded pretty sweet. He said it was worth between $400 and $500. Now, that was more like it.

I asked him if he would play something on his best guitar. Nonchalantly, he said it was the one he had just finished making. He played Debussy's gorgeously melodic "Girl With the Flaxen Hair." On the piano it is fiendishly difficult, with six flats. On the guitar, I cannot imagine. His guitar sang with resonant, clear notes, filling his sizable workshop. Oh, for a guitar like that. How much? "$11,500. Here, do you want to play it?" I shrank back from even touching such an exquisite instrument. I said no because I was too embarrassed to say I no longer knew how to play. And I knew I would be disappointed in my own guitar. He offered that it might take a year or two to sell but there would be a buyer one day. He has a national reputation.

I decided to buy new strings for my Yairi and found the aptly-named Guitar World in Emeryville. Hundreds and hundreds of guitars of all sorts are mounted floor to ceiling on the walls of several large rooms. So many guitar-shoppers it was hard to find a sales person. Who knew? It's worth a trip just to see the place.

I wanted to take advantage of any technological advancements in classical guitar strings in the past decades, so I bought new ones—the best they sold. I can tune accurately with my new $20 digital tuner gadget. I replaced the old, rickety guitar rest with a new one which gently cradles the revived instrument on cushioned arms. I have clipped the nails on my left hand.

Secretly, I hoped my wooing with lovely new strings and a cushioned stand would make my guitar yield her music to me more easily. She has not, and I knew that. She's just as stubborn as ever, withholding a nice, clear chord. I also knew that I was kidding myself that I would go back to playing after so long, and now with one crooked finger. Someday I'll call the luthier again. I'm hoping he'll sell my guitar for me, with all her new accessories. Yet my guitar continues to sit in the closet, in a very nice case. I think of its seductive flamenco rhythms, the lure of folk music, the way it enriches my voice . . . . I could sing like Joan Baez. I could sing like Judy Collins.

I can't bear to sell my guitar.

## The Jewelry Store

I visited Neil's Jewellery and Exchange in a tug-of-war with myself, knowing I would succumb and buy a piece of jewelry. I could hear my mother intoning from the grave, or actually the crematorium, her often-heard warning—a fool and his money are soon parted. I knew I would probably be the fool.

My mother saw danger in all passions, from chocolate (she always divided a candy bar into three pieces for us kids) to giggling ("That's enough now!") to sex ("Carol, we trust you," implying I would not dare shame my family by getting pregnant in high school). Yet later she urged me to buy expensive shoes I could barely afford when we were in Paris. I bought those shoes. I now know that self-indulgent pleasure eventually cancels guilt.

In April 2013, I was in Naples, Florida, with friend Kathleen where we took an air boat ride through the tannin-stained water of the Everglades and were bumped by a huge alligator, cruised and swam in the Gulf, combed for shells on the beach, and pretended revulsion at the beach-front McMansions of the migrating super-rich. Her family has owned two condos there for years. She said, "We used to be the rich people in Naples, but now we are just ordinary."

I had heard a lot about the jewelry store owned by Kathleen's sister and husband. It was the source of Kathleen's considerable collection of jewelry—big stones, real stones.

Their store was not on one of the main shopping streets lined with expensive boutiques but in a strip mall several miles away. Nothing to lure the shopper in except a prominent sign reading, "Neil's Jewellery and Exchange. We buy gold. Consignments." It looked more like a pawn shop than a jewelry store. Knowing I was deceiving myself, I thought we would spend half an hour there and then go back to the beach.

I was surprised to find the place crowded with customers. I could hardly find space at the counter. There were no erect, black-flocked fingers displaying rings in the glass case, no elegant, headless necks wearing tasteful gold chokers. The only organization was a jumble of gold at one end of the glass case, silver in the middle, and gold again at the other end. The jewelry lay in a jumble, loosely organized by silver, gold, and color of stone.

Jewelry lust has a particular kind of energy. Voices hushed, gold weighed, prices discreetly discussed. I trolled the glass counters and, as pins and rings came into focus, I saw treasures. Big heavy necklaces and bracelets of eighteen-karat gold. Diamond bracelets. A ruby section. A sapphire section. An emerald section. The wealthy of Naples bring in their jewelry to sell, consign or exchange. This is a booming business.

Our thirty-minute visit stretched to over two hours because we had to wait out several tropical downpours flooding the parking lot. Two hours in a jewelry store is too long. I began to feel a little ill from the sour smell of tarnished silver. Out of boredom I went back and forth along the counter until something called to me, as I knew it would, and I bought a six-karat pink tourmaline pendant.

Kathleen's niece Caroline tended the counter with her parents. She will inherit the business. She looks the stereotype of a drug dealer's girlfriend. Her shoulder-length hair is dyed jet black, the last third a wide band of bleached white. She wore leggings and a tight short skirt over her stocky body. Her nose and ears were pierced. Several rings on each hand, a heavy gold necklace, and bulky bracelets on each wrist. Her bloat of jewelry looked like inexpensive costume jewelry. But it was all real. Large diamonds in her ears and nose. Overweight gold necklace and bracelets, diamonds and emeralds in her rings. She knows the business but doesn't look like a jeweler. But then the store doesn't look like a jewelry store either.

If my mother had been stuck with me at Neil's Jewellery and Exchange for two hours, I think she would have succumbed too. I would have urged her on.

SATURDAY

They emerged from their homes in twos, threes, fours, and more, all heading in the same direction. I felt connected to everyone I saw. I knew where they were going. Other Saturdays when I see people walking by on the street, I don't know anything about them or their errands. They remain strangers and I remain isolated. This Saturday no one was a stranger, and I felt connected. Each small knot of people flowed into others to form a stream which joined other streams until there was a river of people moving slowly toward the plaza. Some came by bicycle, some by stroller. Others moved by walker and wheelchair. The wave of goodwill grew as more streams converged at the plaza and spilled into the streets for many blocks. It was a happy crowd with a serious mission. We were not there to fight or protest. We were there to see our numbers, to gauge our strength. The fight will come later. That Saturday we were there to celebrate ourselves at the Women's March on January 21, 2017, the day after Donald Trump was inaugurated.

We were there to laugh. For a small donation you could throw a raw egg at a Donald Trump impersonator. A woman wore a huge black spider hat with Trump's face on the body and names of his cabinet picks at the end of each long, hairy leg. A sea of pink "pussy hats." A woman holding a sign, "This pussy grabs back." The Empathy Tent's motto, "You talk, we listen." It was empty that day. It will be useful later.

A trio of aerial dancers emerged from the tenth floor window of City Hall and danced down the façade, secured by lines.

Music and speeches and then threading our way through the tight crowd to a BART station. No hope of boarding a train or even entering a station. I decided to walk. I talked to a young couple who eased my trek for a few blocks. I walked from 14th Street to the Rockridge BART station and then six more blocks up to Broadway, probably five miles. It was a fitting way to commemorate an historic day.

I've been wondering why family members keep secrets from each other. Recently, I got my hand slapped when I revealed a secret. I suppose I did deserve the rebuke. My cousin called to vent about her mother. She was very worried about the level of her mother's stress. She said her mother was even taking an antianxiety medication. This is heresy in that branch of the family. They hold that no one needs to take medication, so it was practically treasonous that my aunt was taking something to help calm her. My cousin added at the end of our conversation that her mother had taken a pill, fell asleep at her computer and could not remember going to bed that night. "But don't say anything about that. Promise you won't say anything about what I've told you." I promised. But I broke my promise when I worried that my aunt's medication was not the right stuff for her and she should tell her doctor. I left this message on her answering machine.

All hell broke loose. Aunt was furious with my cousin for telling me. My cousin was furious with me for calling her mom. She said she could no longer trust me.

When the dust settled and the sting wore off, I thought about what had happened. What was so awful about my knowing that my aunt had had a memory lapse?

I am so miffed about family secrets that next time one of them says, "Now, don't say anything to anyone," I will say, self-righteously, "I don't want to hear it if it's a secret." But then I wouldn't be in on any of the family gossip. And I wouldn't have any juicy secrets to tell.

## MY HEROES

When "My Hero" was suggested as a writing exercise in our writing group, I drew a blank. I didn't have a hero. I worried that meant I admired no one. I stewed about it and out of the stew surfaced my hero. Not one but two; not a hero but heroines. The heroines were too close to recognize. My sisters.

Sharon, the youngest of us three sisters, lived only blocks from the senior facility that, somehow, agreed to take our mother who was declining rapidly into the madness of Alzheimer's. The place didn't provide the cruelly-named "memory care." They admitted our mother anyway who wandered the halls, frantically looking for her mind.

Sharon went to see Mother every day. At first she took her on outings and later she talked to her, sang to her, read to her, reminded her who she was. Anything to tether her to the real world. Near the end she could eat little. The last time I saw her I fed her strawberry ice cream, her favorite. Most of it dribbled down her chin.

Of course, all of Sharon's love and care could not stop the terrible progression of Alzheimer's. But I very much admire her courage, her dedication, her love for our mother. As the youngest of us three daughters, she was often disregarded. With Mother, she faced the terrible and waded right into it. If it was frightening she did not say. She just did it. She was strong in ways none of us had seen. I wonder if I would have been as brave.

Mother died in the night and Sharon went over about 2:00 a.m. She told me she just held Mother, rocked her and told her she would be all right. I know she was right.

She is my hero.

My sister Patti is my hero. She nursed her husband of almost fifty years through three years of undiagnosed deterioration which finally was identified as ALS, Lou Gehrig's disease. How tragic he would be afflicted with such a terrible disease. His football scholarships made it possible for him to go to school. He played college football and then pro for the Detroit Lions for a short time. He sustained several concussions. Today medical researchers are finding a link between concussions and later development of ALS.

His doctors didn't know what was causing his decline. Abdominal surgery to remove a growth. Full recovery. Joy. Then slight slurring of speech. Then difficulty swallowing. Then a feeding tube. Then no speech. My sister mopped up the cups and cups of unswallowed saliva. The horror of ALS is that the mind is unaffected. The body stops working and you are imprisoned within it.

When his doctor told him he had two months to live he jerked in his chair at the words. He was hearing his death sentence. He, too, bore his illness heroically.

She tended him. She mixed the mash and fed him through the feeding tube to keep him alive. He could still climb unaided up the stairs to their bedroom the day he died.

He died just short of their fiftieth wedding anniversary. So did my father; my mother could not celebrate hers either. What would the ancient Roman augurs say about that?

My sister did what she had to do for her husband. I don't know if she complained about it, screamed about it, sobbed about it. She plodded on, doing what she had to do, blending all the horrible, gray glop that went into a feeding tube as though she were preparing dinner as usual. Speaking for him, interpreting for him.

She tended him and after he died, said, quietly, how relieved she was. The end of a long ordeal endured with grace.

She is my hero.

I took advantage of a wonderful opportunity to practice paranoia recently. That's a skill you have to keep sharp or you can lapse into gullibility.

I was more or less accused of stealing a piece of jewelry from the fundraiser where I volunteer. I admired it on Monday, discussed a discount on the high price and went home. Three days later I got a call from Cochair No. 1, Susan Suspicious, that went like this: "Carol, you are interested in the turquoise necklace?" "Well, maybe, depending on the price." "It's missing."

The implied accusation. Hers was not a question: "Do you know where it might be? We can't find it." Just a flat statement. I was calm on the phone and suggested solutions—it was either sold or stolen. "No, nobody remembers selling it." I suggested that Cochair No 2, Friendly Focaccia, might have taken it out for appraisal. Suspicious Susan ended the call abruptly. It was two o'clock and she was ringing up last minute customers. I know she was really busy. But her abrupt hang-up gave me one more reason to pump up my paranoia. Now I was under a cloud of suspicion of theft. You can't prove a negative. Paranoia rising. I was getting a good workout. Paranoia is very useful as a deterrent to a good night's sleep, just in case you might be over-indulging there.

Being accused is bench-pressing a hundred pounds. Building big paranoid muscles. I was on mental overdrive. I thought I might have been set up. That was it! Earlier, when I was working, Cochair

No. 3, Grumpy Gertelbein, would not look at me, would not answer my questions or would snap at me with short answers. One day she sharply ordered me to stop writing up a purchase because it was two o'clock and we were closing. I quietly said I've started this ticket and I'll just finish this one. She had been cold ever since. Was it possible she hid the necklace to get me into trouble and "fired?"

I left a message with Cochair No 2, Friendly Focaccia, to explain the last time I saw the missing piece and hinted I might be being set up and to call me if she wanted to know more. Thank God she did not call back.

Later, friend Jane had wise counsel for me. She advised I talk directly with Cochair No. 3, Grumpy Gertelbein. Of course that was the right action, but then I could not have gone through this vigorous workout on my paranoia.

I was quaking but I called Grumpy Gertelbein whom I thought I had offended. She answered and we had a very friendly conversation. She wasn't grumpy at all. Said she did not remember telling me to stop writing the ticket. No she was not offended. I asked her advice about how to handle the cloud of suspicion. She said not to worry about it. There are usually several instances every year when jewelry disappears. Don't worry, just forget about it. I then asked her if she knew who she was talking to. She said she did not. I said I would reintroduce myself when we next met. That should be interesting. She didn't know who she had struck a peace with. The next time I saw her there was a flicker of a smile and then she went back to the glares and coldness. The peace did not hold. I have no idea what I did to offend her.

When I heard the turquoise necklace was never found, I wanted it more than ever.

My personal session with paranoia was over but a few days later I got an assist from the Oscars when I heard the best picture award went to the wrong picture. Hmmm, was there someone at the Academy who did not like so many awards going to African-American actors?

See how easy paranoia is? It's not hard at all, and if you work at it you'll stay in great shape.

## Dancing into the There There

I cut loose not long after I crossed the border moving from Oregon to California. California symbolized freedom and a new life, so one of the first things I did was lose my virginity at age twenty-five. It wasn't from lack of opportunity earlier. I was too close geographically to my parents who I thought would know if I had sex, so I had to move away before I could start my adult life. It was pre-pill time, another effective restraint on the libido. So, what did I do after I crossed the border into freedom from parental restraints? I got pregnant the first time I had sex.

I cut loose another time much later. Warren (the rageaholic but before he began to rage) and I were driving down Highway 80 near Berkeley on a hot summer's night in his new white Toyota pickup, windows down, wind in our hair. I felt so good I whipped off my t-shirt and rode topless most of the way home. Warren just spluttered and peeked at me sideways. I was slender and didn't feel at all self-conscious. I wanted to feel the wind on my body. I wanted to be reckless yet safe, and I wanted to shake up Warren. It felt almost as good as dancing under strobe lights where your body seems to be cut into geometric pieces that fly all over the room. It felt as good as dancing semi-nude in body paint at the attic party in the Haight.

Cutting loose for me seems to be about being naked and dancing. That is a lot more fun than thinking about which senior residence I'll eventually move into. Maybe I can find a graduated-care unit that offers nude dancing with strobe lights.

## Acknowledgements

Laura Miller deserves my heartfelt gratitude first for encouraging me and then for guiding me through the editorial and technical complexities of producing this book. I could not have done it without her. She is skillful at writing, editing, layout, and design. A Renaissance woman of the word.

Judith Horstman, a journalist and author of seven books, insisted on meticulous fact-checking. She encouraged me when she said, "There's some good stuff in here." High praise coming from one as published as she is.

Mary Ellen McKey noticed too many "ands," which I pared down.

Francie Chan read my manuscript and offered to do it a second time. Once was generous enough.

Thanks to members of my writing group and other readers, all honest, insightful, and supportive: Laura, Francie, Jan, Lisa, Melinda, Jane, Sari, Susanne, and members of Margaret's writing group.

## ABOUT THE AUTHOR

Carol Wolleson was born in Alaska, raised in Oregon, and has lived in the Bay Area since the 1960s. She has been a psychotherapist for the past thirty years. This is her first book. She lives in Oakland, California.